the psychological manager

improve your performance conversations

acknowledgements

There are many people I would like to thank. Firstly, and most importantly, my lovely wife Celia for her undying faith in my modest abilities. Secondly, my ex-colleagues and current friends who have motivated me, inspired me, and feigned interest at this book's progress. And thirdly, the managers I have had and the people I have managed. I learned a lot from you.

Finally, I'd also like to say thank you to Amanda Crook who has beautifully edited and designed this book. Any errors are purely mine.

www.thepsychologicalmanager.com

ISBN 978-1-4710-5999-5

Published in the UK by Lulu.com

Edited and designed by Amanda Crook (www.clarityediting.co.uk)

Cover photo © Peter Storr

the psychological manager

improve your performance conversations

peter storr

about the author

I am a Chartered Psychologist with 30 years of organisational experience. I've led both large and small teams in the private and public sectors and have many years' experience as a management coach. I've spent many years as an external management consultant and at the BBC as an internal Occupational Psychology consultant. Most recently I was strategic Head of Organisation Development at a London-based Russell Group university.

My expertise is centred on management and leadership: helping managers to lead and manage individuals and teams, designing and running managerial assessment and development centres, coaching and coaching training, group facilitation and designing management development programmes. I'm married, live in Berkshire and eventually would like to grow chickens.

I now run my own consultancy, dealing with all aspects of management and team development, assessment and management development project work.

Please contact me at **thepsychologicalmanager@gmail.com** or you can also visit **www.thepsychologicalmanager.com** to let me know what you think of this book, or just to say hello.

contents

foreword

by Dr Paul Brewerton

Not too long ago, I was facilitating a session with a team of executives from a well-known financial services company. They were keen to develop a positive sense of identity within their business division. This, they believed, would help drive up engagement, retention, financial performance and all those other important metrics that businesses are concerned about these days.

Once the group had all agreed that this was a useful avenue to explore, they started to ask questions. Questions like ...

- 'What motivates people to form groups and what are the causes of tribalism?'
- 'How do we get today's generation to really engage with who we are and what we stand for?'
- 'Why don't our managers pass down the messages in the way that we want them to?'
- 'Why is it that we have some standout teams in the division and some that just never seem to get out of second gear?'

- 'What do we need to do differently as leaders and as a team that will help the people out there "get it"?'
- 'Why can't we just come up with a really appealing strapline as a leadership team and send it down the line – surely that will get people more bought in and engaged?'

And so on and so on. So, as these sessions usually go, I tried to help answer some of their questions. As a psychologist, I'm biased. The 'lens' I use to respond to questions like these most typically draws on psychology (and psychology itself borrows heavily from sociology, neurology, anthropology and other disciplines). But it strikes me that psychology has a lot to give the world of work in shining a light on many of the issues raised by this group of senior managers.

The group were genuinely surprised by some of the answers I gave and by the different directions that this took the discussion as they mapped out their action plan. I'm hopeful that providing some insights from psychology helped them to develop a plan that reflected some of the idiosyncrasies, complexities and realities of human nature, so that they had a better chance of genuinely engaging their people through change.

I am also hopeful that their people will therefore come out the other side of change better able to make sense of their division and their place in it, feeling more motivated and more positive about their organisation and their contribution to it.

All too often, though, psychology can appear as a bit of a mystical 'dark art' that holds something of value, although we're not quite sure what.

I first met Peter Storr at a five-day training event that he was running for HR professionals on the appropriate use of psychometric tests in the workplace. Not the most fascinating of topics, is it? But Pete had a way of putting across the key points from the training that had his audience engrossed from the beginning to end of each training day.

Perhaps what kept his audience interested was his storytelling and his anecdotes, which were invariably entertaining, often personal and always relevant to the material. Or maybe it was his expansive knowledge of psychology and the little nuggets of research he threw in to the mix throughout the day that left the audience wanting more. Perhaps it was his dry sense of humour that kept them on their toes. Or maybe it was the combination of all these things, alongside a deep understanding of his material that made for such a rich learning environment for delegates.

I left the event feeling inspired and apprehensive in equal measure, knowing that it would be me taking the next group of delegates through the same training that I'd just watched Pete waltz through, and feeling that I could never deliver the material as well as that.

So here we are, 15 years later, and I find myself in a similar place, reading through Pete's book, *The Psychological Manager: Improve Your Performance Conversations*, frankly feeling gobsmacked that he's been able to translate his engaging delivery style to book form (how did he do that?).

I'm also struck by the way that Pete has put together a book that takes the reader on a journey of discovery that starts by giving us a better understanding of ourselves. Then he gives us some great insights on how to have conversations with the individuals in our teams and about how teams work. Through this, he builds our knowledge of the psychology and behaviour of whole organisations. And all through the eyes of today's managers and leaders.

For me, this book does something that very few others have. It translates the hard-to-reach corners of psychology and social science research into tangible, useful tools for today's managers. And on top of that, it's a right fun read.

My recommendation is that all financial services executives (and all other managers, too) get hold of a copy and keep it close by. You never know when you'll need to solve the next messy people-puzzle in your organisation.

Dr Paul Brewerton is a prominent Occupational Psychologist and Associate Fellow of the British Psychological Society, specialising in the application of strengths and positive psychology in the workplace to drive up engagement and performance at work.

He has published numerous books, chapters and conference papers on topics such as organisational culture, the psychological contract, organisational research methods, strengths psychology and psychometric test design, and convened the CIPD's postgraduate course on the Psychology of Management for many years.

Dr Brewerton has been leading successful consulting practices for 15 years, including Blue Edge and, more recently, Strengths Partnership, with a focus on developing individuals, teams and organisations to achieve their potential through better understanding of the psychology that drives human behaviour at work.

introduction

We've all met some pretty rubbish managers of people. Unusual way to start a book, I'll grant you, but it's true. And although I have seen some great management behaviours in my time (which I hope I've honoured by copying), I've probably learnt more from seeing it done really, really badly – and then doing the opposite.

As a manager, I believe passionately in the importance and value of role-modelling – setting an example of what behaviours we wish to see around us by doing them ourselves.

I could go on for a long time about the lack of consistency, vision or ambition in those 'inverse role models', but it strikes me that most of the poor management practice I've been subjected to or observed as a consultant can be condensed to being the result of two main things:

- managers who treat managing people as something to do if they have time once the day job is done. The trouble is that the day job never gets done, so neither does the people management. Staff are left floundering by an absent manager who has little sense of direction or cohesion.

- managers who seem averse to having real, honest *conversations* with their staff. They behave as if the people working for them are not actually human, but merely people-shaped resources that happen to have a job description.

So the *attitude* – seeing managing people as an important part of your job – and the *skills* – having structured and meaningful performance conversations with your staff – is the focus of this book.

I believe that psychology has a lot to say about people management, and a basic knowledge of the relevant theories can help you to become a **Psychological Manager** – using that knowledge to become a better manager of people. And if you do it properly, you'll be amply repaid for any of the time and effort you put in to building relationships and having meaningful conversations with the people you manage.

Behind any set of skills is some background knowledge, and in this book I've summarised some of the relevant psychological theories so that – with practice – you can have better performance and development conversations with your staff.

In writing this book I've been influenced by three main sources, which together I believe have given me a pretty clear idea of what managing people should be about:

- an up-to-date knowledge of psychological theory from my own studies as an Occupational Psychologist, subsequent reading and continuing professional development
- my work on management development programmes as a designer, trainer, facilitator and coach
- my own experiences as a manager and of being managed.

Throughout my career I've come across many people who have questions, concerns and lack of confidence when having those sometimes difficult staff performance conversations. This book is for those people and everyone like them – which is most of us. I hope you find it useful.

Peter Storr
C.Psychol
January 2012

section

one

why become a psychological manager?

• 1 • the benefits of using psychology • 2 • a (very) brief history of psychology •

chapter 1

the benefits of using psychology

It's my firm belief that psychology is not for psychologists. Actually, it is, but what I mean is that it shouldn't *just* be for them. Nor should psychology just be knowledge for knowledge's sake – you have to be able to do something with it.

In this book I've tried to provide enough theory to give a decent grounding in some of the key psychological theories that relate to people management. By becoming a Psychological Manager – using a knowledge of psychology to have structured, meaningful and insightful performance conversations with your staff – you can make a huge difference to your success as a manager.

And by understanding both the theory and practice of performance-based conversations in goal setting, feedback, coaching and motivation – and also what happens when a collection of individuals become a team – you will become a better manager of people.

Most of the bad managers I've met have been ones who were unable to have these performance conversations, focusing instead only on more tangible things such as budgets and managing projects. Important stuff. But you can't do any of it properly without building relationships, and you can't build relationships without having meaningful conversations.

So although this book is written by a psychologist with psychology at its core, it's not meant for other psychologists[1]. Instead it's meant for managers who want to know how to interact with their staff in a more constructive, focused and *human* way. Part of a manager's job is to understand others' motivations and personality foibles, and a basic knowledge of psychological theory will help you to do so. Learn what the magician knows and it is no longer magic.

I've been constantly surprised over the years at the lack of support many managers get when they suddenly start managing people, instead of merely things or their own workload. People are messy; they have messy thoughts and messy feelings, and managers have to deal not only with their own feelings, but also with their team members' feelings as well. Excellent managers don't just deal with them, however; they have the understanding of why the thoughts and feelings may be there, and have some tools and techniques to guide them through to get the best possible performance – and ongoing development – out of their team.

By understanding and practising the tools, techniques and attitudes in this book – by being a Psychological Manager – you will have the potential to be a truly excellent manager of people. Reading this book is the first step – the rest is just practice.

finding your way around

section one why become a psychological manager?

We start with this brief introductory Section one, which includes a potted history of psychology over the last 100 years. Many of the major psychological theories and approaches that we look at here are revisited throughout the book, particularly as we learn about the world of individual differences in Section three.

section two building you: personal development

Section two is about your own managerial journey. After all, there's no point expecting your staff to be self aware, respond to feedback and have a focus on

1 Although bizarrely, in my experience many psychologists are rubbish managers, despite knowing better. Never buy a plumber's house ...

development if you're not doing it too. This section forms a backdrop to the rest of the book, and looks at *why* you should focus on your own development, how to determine *what* to develop, and gives some initial ideas as to the *how*.

section three we are all the same. but different

The third section explores the world of individual differences, with separate chapters on intelligence, personality, beliefs, attitudes and knowledge, and motivation – the key psychological constructs that make us different from one another.

section four building skill and dealing with will: facilitating performance and development

Section four is about building the skill of the individuals in your team, and examines some of the key conversational skills of performance management – goal setting, giving feedback and coaching. We also focus on how to motivate individual team members – dealing with will – and use the skill/will matrix to determine the most beneficial style of management for a particular individual at a particular time.

section five building your team: understanding and managing

The final section turns the spotlight on the team: how teams are formed, group psychology, high performing teams, and how to manage virtual teams. We also look at the importance of focusing on the *process* of team activity, as opposed to merely the *content*, and describe six facilitation techniques to help you get the best out of your team's time together.

Where relevant, at the end of each section you'll find a summary and a checklist of what you – as a Psychological Manager – can do to ensure that you're getting the best performance out of yourself, the individuals who report to you and the team that you are responsible for.

If you can achieve most of the points on the checklist you'll not only help to shape your organisation's culture, but will also role-model and reinforce good practice. And you'll be a far better people manager than most. Your team – and your own boss – will thank you for it.

chapter 2

a (very) brief history of psychology

Understanding the history and 'journey' of psychological thought (or *paradigms*) has helped me to navigate a route map through the major theories – especially when it comes to the world of individual differences (Section three). These paradigms were ways of looking at the world – what were perceived at the time as fundamental truths, and what linked the great thoughts of the time together. What's interesting is that they are all still very much current and in use in various guises. So no paradigm is any more 'right' than any of the others.

To illustrate, let's take the example of an individual entering therapy to deal with a particular stressful life event:

- Freudian psychoanalytic therapy looks back in time to unresolved childhood stages and anxieties[1], the various defence mechanisms that have arisen as a consequence and, in some cases, why and how you drew (unconsciously) that life event to you in the first place.

1 If it's not one thing, it's a mother.

- Humanistic therapy focuses more on our freedom to choose our responses to life's pressures (instead of them being channelled by drives and motives of which we are unaware) and that, with empathic understanding by the therapist, we will find our own individual way through our problems through acceptance of our own responsibilities.
- Cognitive behavioural therapy looks at our perceptions and thought processes about the event itself; while we can't change the fact that the event happened, it occurred in the past and we can change how we think about it in the here and now – often by challenging irrational beliefs that we may hold (such as 'I can never cope with traumas like these').

All of these approaches have merit, have been shown to have successful outcomes (though not without some sceptical challenges) and may even be combined in a more eclectic approach to therapy. Some conditions may be synonymous with a particular form of therapy (phobias with cognitive behavioural approaches, for example) but by and large, they are all equally valid[2].

Approaches to therapy are obviously only one manifestation of the sequence of paradigm shifts (the other main one we'll be looking at later is the world of motivation theory in Chapter 10) but they appear to symbolise the essence of each one. The sequence also gives the appearance at least of each one being an antidote to the preceding one. While this isn't technically correct – and many paradigms were 'out there' concurrently – it's still a useful way of thinking about them.

the psychodynamic approach

Many writers believe that the 'science' of psychology starts with Freud and his book *The Interpretation of Dreams* (1899). In it he introduces the concepts of the unconscious and the Oedipus complex, blending literary and psychological analysis. To Freud and the later psychodynamic psychologists (the name given to this school of thought), we are ruled by our unconscious motives and (often sexual) drives, which means we ourselves can't give an account of them – they have to be analysed and interpreted through analysis.

The focus is very much on the past – on the negative thoughts and feelings that we protect ourselves from through defence mechanisms such as repression

---

2 Some writers have drawn parallels with religion; there are many different types, but all are attempting to address similar issues. I guess psychology has started fewer wars, though.

and projection, and their effects on present anxiety states and other disorders. Other later writers in this paradigm (Carl Jung, for example) reduce the emphasis on the sexual element, but the essence of the unconscious shaping our lives remains.

One of the major problems with this paradigm is that most of the central tenets are untestable – as soon as you attempt to prove they don't exist, you can be accused of repressing or denying them! These processes cannot be independently observed, and can be interpreted only by fully trained psychoanalysts – hardly the most unbiased group of people after undergoing at least five years of training. The impact of Freud, however, was and is still huge – and the science of psychology was born.

the behaviourist approach

But to one group of writers and theorists the psychodynamic approach wasn't quite scientific enough. The behaviourist school sought to change all that. If what defined the psychodynamic school was introspection and subjective interpretation, what defined the behaviourists was scientific rigour and objective experimentation[3].

John Watson was pretty much a contemporary of Freud, but their approaches were polar opposites. The essence of behaviourism is that our behaviour is learned through reinforcement – we do what we've been encouraged to do and what our environment rewards us for doing; our environment gives us a stimulus, and we respond accordingly depending on our past history of that stimulus. The concept of the 'autonomous man' is utterly rejected; we are the product of our environmental reinforcements.

What is unknown and untestable – and therefore not the remit of scientific endeavour – is what is in between the stimulus and response, such as physiology, thoughts and feelings. So according to the major theorists in this area (Watson, B.F. Skinner and Edward Thorndike), the study of behaviour should be a natural science, akin to biology or physics, without the need for hypothetical inner states of mind complicating matters.

When we train a dog, we're using the core tools (reinforcement and punishment) of Skinner's concept of operant conditioning. The same is true when we 'train' a child into positive behaviour by rewarding it, or punishing

3 Although it was mainly with pigeons and rats. And Pavlov's dogs if you go back far enough.

bad behaviour. For more complex levels of human functioning, many found the behaviourist approach to be wanting; it was the messy bit in between the stimulus and response (thoughts, perceptions and feelings) that was deemed worthy of study once we got halfway through the twentieth century.

the cognitive approach

The whole point and focus of the cognitive approach was this internal world of mental processes. Ignoring the bit in the middle between a stimulus and our subsequent actions oversimplified the complex nature of the human condition. Like the behaviourists, the cognitive theorists tended to reject the unscientific approach of the psychodynamic school and embraced the scientific method.

But unlike the behaviourists they saw the internal processes – that you may not be able to physically observe but are there anyway – as fair game for study. It's no coincidence that this period (the 1950s and 60s) also saw the rise of the early computers; many analogies were drawn between our internal mental processes and with the internal computational processes of the computer.

Cognitive researchers (early ones included Noam Chomsky, Donald Broadbent and Frederic Bartlett, but there are plenty still around) focus on the inner world of perception – for example, whether we build up a representation of our world from the data (bottom-up processing) or apply existing models to data (top-down) to make sense of it. They look at the different forms of memory and attention; linguistics and language acquisition and thinking processes such as logic and judgement.

What we think and perceive affects how we feel, so cognitive approaches to therapy centre around changing our thoughts and perceptions of a past or present issue to modify our current feelings.

the humanist approach

At the same time as the cognitive scientists were formulating their early theories, another school of thought was challenging the 'controlled by our unconscious childlike desires' approach of the psychodynamic theorists, and the simplistic mechanism of learned behaviour of the behaviourists. The humanists drew on the field of existentialist thought (Kierkegaard, Nietzsche) and eastern philosophy, taking a more holistic view of the human condition.

The early proponents, such as Abraham Maslow and Carl Rogers, argued that psychology should focus on what it means to be human; our self image, our dreams and ideals, and our individuality – our internal frame of reference. Theirs is a far more rosy view of human nature in that we are essentially free, responsible human beings who strive to become the best people we are capable of being, through our own choices. Human nature is constructive, forward-moving, realistic and trustworthy. Research and the experimental method featured heavily, but in a more qualitative as opposed to quantitative way; a phenomenological methodology – one that seeks to understand an individual's subjective experience of the world.

Many coaching and therapeutic models[4] are based on the client-centred approach developed by Rogers, and the humanist movement as a whole is largely responsible for the plethora of self help books in your local bookshop. The key essence of all of these models is that we are in control of our own destiny, and through self awareness we can discover what we are in control over and identify our own solutions to our problems, in order to self actualise[5] into a fully functioning human being.

the psychobiological approach

While this is less of a paradigm or coherent school of thought than the others, the psychobiological approach is where modern research techniques are adding the most up-to-date knowledge about how we operate. This is the study of nerve cells, of brain circuits and neurotransmitters and genetic components of behaviour.

The principle is not new; William James in the nineteenth century extolled the virtues of understanding biological structures as a way of understanding our behaviour. What *is* new is the world of Electroencephalography (EEG), Magnetoencephalography (MEG) and functional Magnetic Resonance Imaging (fMRI) scanning capabilities.

These techniques can measure precise blood flow and electrical activity in specific parts of the brain that may be being used for particular activities, or under certain circumstances or disorders. They have applications for research

4 The GROW model of coaching we explore in Chapter 13 is largely derived from Rogerian principles.

5 The actualising tendency is life's master motive, according to the humanists.

into consciousness, memory and decision making, perception and emotion, as well as when it's all going wrong – Parkinson's, Alzheimer's, autism and anxiety.

This research has started to infiltrate the world of business writing – we now can see what happens to our limbic system when we get insights, when we're being coached, and when we're working in teams; we can see the mirroring of electrical impulses when we unconsciously share emotions and we see the effects on our hormone levels when we receive positive feedback and social acceptance.

the positive psychology approach

Finally, let's go back to another paradigm shift, albeit not one universally accepted. However, it is one that's currently gaining ground in the world of work and one that resonates with the ideals behind this book.

You'll remember that the humanists took a rather more positive view of the human condition and suggested that we are all striving to be the best we can be. The positive psychology movement goes back to this idea[6] to suggest that psychology should also be about nurturing talent, promoting happiness and making life more fulfilling.

Two writers stand out – Mihaly Csikszentmihalyi, who promotes the concept of flow (when we are at our best, being absorbed in the moment with just the right amount of challenge), and Martin Seligman. Seligman was famous for electrocuting dogs in the 1960s[7], but in the late 1990s was suggesting that psychology was preoccupied with mental illness, and if it chose it had rather a lot to offer the world in terms of happiness and fulfilment.

A recent discovery about happiness may illustrate the point (aided by the psychobiological approach, in that we can now see this happening). When we think about a scenario, we default to the strongest, most reinforced neural

6 Also the focus of the Enlightenment and before that the Ancient Greeks. It's not a new idea.

7 This may need some context. I don't think he was doing it just for fun. He found that if he provided a way of stopping the electric shock – say, by pressing a lever – the dogs soon learned this and stopped it. If the lever didn't work, the dogs soon learned that they could not control the shocks and, basically, gave up and lay there being zapped. Not surprisingly they exhibited signs of depression, which Seligman suggested was caused by the concept of *learned helplessness*. This is still a well respected explanation of some depressive states – we need to have the perception of control to function healthily. Of course, if we can learn to be helpless, we can also learn to be optimistic – and this is where positive psychology comes in.

pathway. If this is a pessimistic pathway, it gets reinforced again, and over time becomes our normal way of thinking. In our discussion of the *Six Thinking Hats* © technique of facilitation (see Chapter 20), we talk about the dangers of habitually wearing the Black hat – seeing every situation as negative and tending to look at why something can't be done. However, just as Seligman found that we can learn optimism, we can train ourselves to take the positive view, and with time, practice and reinforcement the positive pathway becomes the default one. Hence the saying 'lucky people get lucky' – they don't, but they just notice it more and take advantage of it[8].

For our purposes then, the positive psychology movement focuses on individuality and capacity for self actualisation and change (as in the humanists) and the identification of – and capitalising on – the strengths we have as individuals to aid confidence and optimal functioning. It has been written about extensively in the organisational development literature (see Chapter 20 regarding appreciative enquiry as a facilitation technique), and in such concepts as authenticity in leadership and strengths-based coaching.

8 The BBC (February 2011) reported on some tentative research that found that our expectations of whether painkillers work affected the outcome – if we didn't expect them to have an effect, they didn't. If patients expected them to work, different parts of the brain lit up and the drugs had more of an effect.

section

two

building you:

personal development

the importance of attitude

In the Introduction I mentioned that one of the most important attributes of a manager is the attitude that managing people is a fundamental part of your job. To a large extent, once you manage a team of people, it *is* your job. The skill bit comes later, and probably won't come at all if the attitude isn't there.

There's another side to the same attitude coin. To be a Psychological Manager, you also need the attitude that your own development is as important as the development of those you manage. There's no point – and it will come across as hypocritical – if you extol the virtues of feedback, coaching and motivation without applying it to yourself too. It's important and necessary – and you deserve it.

There's a third side to this coin[1]. In his book *Teaching Smart People How to Learn*, Chris Argyris argues that bright, successful people (let's assume that's you) are so used to having to be high performing all the time that this results in a natural defensiveness about acknowledging development needs – even to themselves – to avoid threat or feelings of vulnerability. This defensiveness in turn leads to a closed-loop reasoning, where views from outside (i.e. other people) are ignored, rejected or denied. Add to this high aspirations and the result is, in the words of Argyris, *brittle despondency*.

There are two ways out of this defensive quagmire. Clever people are usually analytical, strategic and critical. Argyris suggests that these qualities, when applied to their own development – focusing on data, formulating a strategic plan and being constructively critical of the results – are just what are needed to avoid the quicksand into despondency. In addition, managers need to role-model this behaviour to those below them in the hierarchy if they expect everyone else to do it too.

So now we'll look at three good reasons *why* we should focus on our own development[2].

---

1 Call it the edge if you're going be pedantic about it.

2 Seeing it written down like this makes the answer seem obvious, but I'm asked it time and time again on management courses, and by and large people don't.

chapter 3

the 'why' of personal development

no-one else will

Perhaps the main reason to focus on your own development is that if *you* don't, no-one else will. The concept of career has changed fundamentally in the last 20 or 30 years. The job-for-life has well and truly gone, and therefore so has the idea of security in your employer.

Instead this has been replaced with security in your *employability*, which naturally involves continuous learning and skills development[1]. This is both scary and empowering. In the positive psychology tradition (see Chapter 2), it puts us and our own individuality and strengths in charge of our own career trajectory – whatever that looks like.

People now work for many organisations instead of one or two, and there are often multiple, diverse ways to reach the same point on the ladder. How you

1 When I joined a well-known bank in the 1980s I was told, proudly, that I'd never have to think about my career again. It would all be done for me 'if you keep your nose clean'. I never found out what they meant.

get there is up to you. This puts us in charge of our own destiny, with the responsibility resting firmly with us to develop a portfolio of transferable skills to take from one employer to another.

skills portfolio

Charles Handy[2] has written extensively on this concept of the portfolio career – we build up our personal skills portfolio, like an artist or a model, to show prospective clients. We're essentially saying to that potential employer 'This is who I am, and these are the skills I bring with me if you employ me'. Building this portfolio becomes your responsibility, and what it looks like depends on where you want to end up.

Our CV these days looks quite different from how it looked before; instead of a list of duties we've performed in our various roles, it becomes a description of competencies or skillsets that have helped us achieve our goals, and how they have added value to the organisations we've worked for. According to *The 2020 Workplace*[3] we will be hired and promoted based on our reputation – the brand we've built up through our portfolio of skills and social networks.

technological changes

Technological and economic changes also mean that even if we stay in the same role for a while, it will need to evolve to meet the new challenges or ways of working. Most leadership literature talks about the new skills required of leaders – the ability to manage innovation, ambiguity, constant change and complexity. Change and uncertainty are the new steady and reliable!

As an example, the role and resulting expectations of the line manager currently needs to change with the rise of the virtual team and remote working, as explored in Chapter 18[4]. Even the concept of 'department' within an organisation is taking a bashing, with the increase of cross-functional temporary work teams, brought together to do a specific job and then disbanding again. This calls on different skills (innovation, collaboration, flexibility) than we've previously been used to. We need to remain current and change with (and shape) the changing workplace by developing these core competencies.

---

2 *The Empty Raincoat* and many others.

3 Jeanne C. Meister and Karie Willyerd (2010).

4 Confusingly, there's also a movement to reduce the reliance on technology and get people actually talking to each other instead of a mobile device ...

the Peter Principle

There's also the concept of the Peter Principle[5]. This was originally meant to be a tongue-in-cheek exposé of incompetence, but with regard to management skills it often has an element of truth to it. The principle states that an individual in an organisation will rise to his or her level of incompetence – you do a good job, so you get promoted, etc until you're promoted to a job you can no longer do – and historically (the book was written in the 1960s) you just stayed there. Being rubbish. Workplaces were therefore full of incompetent people who *used* to be good. Classic examples are:

- the excellent teacher or academic who is so good that they end up managing a department (badly) and not doing any teaching
- the IT worker who spends their formative years hacking into websites and then gets a job designing websites, doing so well that they end up leading the team of website designers – with no managerial experience, training or even desire to do so.

So the 'incompetence' is not necessarily the result of the job being more difficult, but rather the fact that it's different – and it's often the management bit that's the different bit[6].

your own managerial development

The way to avoid this happening to you, of course, is to ensure that your development focuses on the managerial part of your job at least as much as any technical development needs.

The stumbling block to all this is often around the fundamental, perhaps most basic psychological bringer of anxiety; loss. Let me explain what I mean by referring to the concept of the Leadership Pipeline[7].

When we start work, we are usually on pipeline (pathway) one – we manage ourselves and our workload. We focus on developing our job-related technical

5 No relation.

6 This is similar to the Dilbert Principle, after the cartoon character, which suggests that incompetent people are promoted to management to prevent them doing any further damage on the shop floor.

7 *The Leadership Pipeline* (2001) by Ram Charan, Stephen Drotter and James Noel.

skills and concentrate on our own results. We then, just like in the description of the Peter Principle above, get promoted based on that past history. This is passage one – the journey from managing ourselves to managing others.

Charan et al suggest that this is where many people start to fail. We naturally want to continue doing what made us successful, and so we find it hard to let go of the day job to concentrate on managing people – we don't make the mindset shift. The bits that get missed are typically setting goals with others, motivating, coaching and managing performance and development.

So there are two things at play here – building and acquiring skills (the focus of Section four) and dealing with the loss of what made you successful in the first place. And when our loss buttons are pressed, we react in the same way as we do to a threat – fight or flight (or a large dose of denial), but rarely with enthusiasm and gusto.

The trick is to value this new type of work as much as what got you there; to treat management skills and attitudes as essential for your own development and future success. And as this 'challenge of the passages' continues up the hierarchy – from managing others to managing managers, right up to CEO where you manage everything[8] – it's always going to be a work in progress.

8 The ones who get it right, according to Charan et al, demonstrate three achievements: defining and assigning the work to be done, enabling it to happen by giving feedback, coaching and providing resources, and building relationships to generate open dialogue and an atmosphere of trust.

chapter 4

the 'what' of personal development

your values and beliefs

When deciding what and how to develop, or even when shaping our careers, one of the common limiting factors is that we often ignore our own value systems. The following simple questions can have complicated answers:

- What are your critical values?
- Where do you want to be in five years?
- What is most important to you in your career?
- What would success in your career look like?
- What would success in your career feel like?
- What essential parts of 'you' do you bring to work?

These are extremely useful questions to think about to get in touch with what you really want from your career. To quote Steve Radcliffe, an experienced leadership coach, good leaders are 'up to something'. Leading is about working out what you want to see in the future, where you want to be and what you want as your legacy. You can't do this effectively without tapping into your belief and value systems. And if you believe that this future is inevitable, it's more likely to happen.

intelligent careers model

Some career coaches separate three components to help their clients focus their development and energy. This is based on the Intelligent Careers model[1]:

- Knowing **why**: getting in touch with your values, motivations and beliefs in relation to work
- Knowing **how**: becoming aware of the skills, knowledge and other qualities that you already have
- Knowing **whom**: embracing the power of networks.

This model is used to empower us to see the choices we have, to understand our own sense of purpose and what we need to do to get there.

self awareness

Of course what's also needed as much as getting in touch with our own value systems is a healthy dose of self awareness. This covers everything from being aware of your own strengths and weaknesses, to how you learn best and in what scenarios, to your own emotional resilience and what pushes your buttons, as it were.

Improving self awareness is usually at the front end of most management development programmes, which may include 360 degree feedback (see Chapter 12), coaching, psychometric assessment and review of preferences, strengths analysis and competency/skills audits. It is one of the core constituents of emotional intelligence models, and to many is the cornerstone of the concept.

emotional intelligence

It's worth saying a few words on the emotional intelligence topic, as it is frequently used as an overarching principle or framework on management development

1 Arthur, Claman and DeFillippi (1995).

programmes. The development of your own emotional intelligence is the element that could have the biggest impact on your success as a people manager, because it contains so many key relational concepts.

There have been many attempts over the last 80 years or so to expand the definition of intelligence (see Section three for a fuller exploration of intellect) to include more social intelligences; perhaps the most often cited is Howard Gardner's work on multiple intelligence[2]. His model included interpersonal intelligence (being able to read others' emotions and motivations) and intrapersonal intelligence (self awareness), because the existing definitions did not adequately explain cognitive functioning in the real world.

There's much fierce debate as to what emotional intelligence actually *is*, with some theorists arguing that it is a cognitive ability (with associated 'tests', like an ability-based IQ test[3]) and others suggesting it is more like a set of personality traits (made popular by writers such as Daniel Goleman). The essence of the concept, however, can pretty much be distilled to some core constructs, regardless of how they're measured:

- **Self awareness**: to be able to recognise your own emotions and why you are feeling them. You realise the link between those feelings and your subsequent behaviour and performance, and recognise their impact on yourself and others.
- **Self control**: to be able to control those emotions and associated impulses[4]. You are able to stay positive and composed in stressful situations and remain calm and focused.

---

2 *Frames of Mind* (1983).

3 Such as the Mayer-Salovey-Caruso Emotional Intelligence Test (MSCEIT).

4 This one was pretty much the starting point for writers like Goleman. Walter Mischel, a psychologist at Stanford in the early 1970s, performed what later became known as the *marshmallow experiment*. He gave four-year-old children a marshmallow, saying that if they could resist temptation for 15 minutes and not eat it immediately, they could have two. About a third of the children could do it, the concept becoming known as *deferred gratification*. This ability to defer gratification in follow-up studies was correlated with higher SATs scores, better health and higher incomes as adults. Goleman calls this ability to delay immediate gratification as one of the most fundamental psychological skills, being at the root of emotional self control. He also suggests that this is learned behaviour and can be developed – something to bear in mind when your four-year-old screams blue murder in the supermarket for a sweet. By putting up with it and giving a sweet when it's more appropriate, you're teaching your child delayed gratification and saving them from prison.

- **Social awareness**: the ability to read and deal appropriately with the emotions of others. You are able to show sensitivity and understanding of others' perspectives – real empathic understanding.

You'll notice that being nice and fluffy just doesn't cut it. Being emotionally intelligent may involve challenging and confronting if that's the most appropriate course of action. It's also not about venting your emotions at every opportunity[5] – it's about managing your emotions intelligently to achieve the outcome you desire or that the situation warrants.

Structurally, the key part of the brain associated with regulating emotions is the limbic system, which includes the amygdala. This appears to be where we store emotional memories; an evolutionary survival trick that helped us shortcut the thinking process when faced with something scary (such as a sabre-toothed cat, for example). Under those circumstances, the ability to react immediately without passing the data through the cortex (the 'thinking' part of the brain) meant that we survived[6].

Today's sabre-toothed cat, however, is an angry customer or an email from the boss – the problem is we're running on 100,000-year-old hardware, so it presses the same buttons. The ability to override the impulse, and react appropriately to the situation, is the emotional intelligence link back to the deferred gratification concept[7].

So what does all this mean for you, the Psychological Manager? If you take the three fundamental constructs of emotional intelligence described above,

---

5 We've all met people who have inappropriate emotional outbursts, and then try to justify them by claiming they're just healthily expressing how they feel. It may be healthy for them, but not necessarily for other people – or, most importantly for emotional intelligence theory, the situation at hand.

6 As opposed to standing there thinking 'Ooo, I wonder what this big orangey-coloured thing with big teeth is?'

7 Recent research has shown a link with a poorly-functioning amygdala and criminality, and it's not hard to understand why. If someone can't resist impulse or delay gratification, then stealing or reacting violently may become the default behaviour. Stephen Fry in his autobiographical book *The Fry Chronicles* puts this far better than I can: 'I was a natural criminal because I lacked just that ability to resist temptation or to defer pleasure for one single second. Whatever guard there is on duty in the minds and moral makeup of the majority had always been absent from his post in my mental barracks' (page 28). A BBC *Horizon* programme (September 2011) explored the link between a poorly functioning amygdala, the MAOA gene (or lack of it) and psychopathy – interestingly, four times more prevalent in the boardroom than in the general population.

it's not hard to see how they map on to the vast majority of management competency frameworks:

- Self awareness relates to issues of confidence and authenticity
- Self control relates to achievement, trustworthiness and credibility
- Social awareness relates to relationship management, empathic understanding of colleagues and clients, influencing and persuasion skills, managing conflict and networking/building relationships.

In *The New Leaders*, Goleman argues that leadership is a relational concept, working through the power of finely tuned emotions – what he calls *resonant leadership*. We are judged as managers not only on our deliverables and goal achievement, but also on our ability to handle ourselves, our relationships and our ability to get the most out of the people who report to us. And as our emotions are contagious – especially so as a manager – how you handle your emotions is closely observed and 'caught' by those around you.

The implication is that working on this part of your development will have a big impact on your abilities as a manager. Being aware of your own interpersonal style and skill levels, and focusing development on them, will pay at least as many dividends as improving your budgetary or project management nous. In this book we focus on the specific *conversational* skills concerned, and techniques for becoming more self aware are the subject of the next chapter.

chapter 5

the 'how' of personal development

why self awareness is important

Self awareness[1] is perhaps the key construct in the myriad of theories relating to emotional intelligence, and is usually the starting point in any development journey. This involves understanding where you are now, thinking about where you want to get to and working out a development plan – which may include capitalising on strengths, rather than merely developing weak points – to get there.

People with strong self awareness are realistic and honest about their strengths and weaknesses and understand – and usually act on – their principles. The best have habituated the practice of periodic quiet reflection to get in touch with both aspirations and current reality. One book used extensively on

1 We're not so much concerned with Descartes' *cogito ergo sum* (I think, therefore I am) of whether you exist or not, but with what you choose to exist to do. For the purposes of this book, you exist.

management development programmes (*Why Should Anyone Be Led by You?*[2]) devotes the first two chapters to these concepts: 'Being yourself – more – with skill' and 'Know and show yourself – enough'.

Let me digress slightly here. There is a concept in the world of organisational development (which may include teambuilding, coaching and counselling, and organisational culture diagnostic work) of 'self as instrument'. Writers and practitioners alike in this field[3] stress the importance of anyone in a helping profession paying attention to themselves – not only to their own development but also in understanding their own reactions to change and ambiguity, control mechanisms and needs, and their need for approval or otherwise – in order to accurately diagnose those needs in others and to successfully intervene[4].

Obviously we're not talking of becoming organisational development consultants or therapists here, but the same principle is true of being a manager. In a way it can be conceptualised as a helping profession. If you are having conversations about motivation, having structured coaching-style conversations, and noticing the psychological effects being in a team has on its members (which you will be by the end of this book), then understanding your own drivers, strengths, styles and foibles will enable you to temporarily put them to one side and increase your ability to be objective. That of which we are unaware controls us!

becoming more self aware

So how do we become more self aware? Undergoing five years of psychoanalytic training should do it, but that is rather extreme (unless you want to become a therapist, of course). Having a coach is perhaps the workplace equivalent and it can be extremely useful in this regard – although this option isn't necessarily available to all of us.

appraisals and SWOT analysis

If you have appraisals then your last few may (depending on the skill of your own manager) reveal something if you look at them in sequence:

---

2 Rob Goffee and Gareth Jones (2006).

3 Mee-Yan Cheung-Judge and Linda Holbeche, *Organisation Development* (2011).

4 Many psychoanalysts in the Freudian tradition argue that they have had so much therapeutic analysis themselves during their qualifications that anything they feel or notice is pure projection from their client. There are many that debate the accuracy (or possibility) of this, however.

- What are the common themes?
- What do they say about your interpersonal or working style?
- What are your strengths and weaknesses?

Could you use the data to help build up a SWOT analysis relating to your own development? Think about the following:

- **Strengths**: What do you do well? What evidence do you have? What personal qualities do you bring to your management? What are you most proud of about you?
- **Weaknesses**: What could you be better at? What don't you handle well? When do you get frustrated? What causes it? What evidence do you have?
- **Opportunities**: What factors external to your own skills and qualities have a positive impact on your management? How can you capitalise on the strengths identified above even further?
- **Threats**: What factors external to you might get in the way? What are the things that may hold you back? What do you have to be wary of in your environment?

managerial competencies

You could also consider doing a structured review of your managerial competencies. If you work somewhere without a managerial competency framework, then you can either make one up, go back to your job description or merely list the qualities and skills needed to do your job – for example:

- handling conflict
- having difficult conversations
- giving feedback
- coaching others.

Rate yourself between **1** (priority for development) and **5** (excellent performance). At the same time, you can review how important these skills are for your current role and see how this informs your development priorities.

personality preferences

Your organisation may be able to arrange some psychometric questionnaires for you as a way of understanding your personality preferences or motivational drivers. In Chapter 19 we discuss many options for you to use with your own team; you need to be prepared to go through the same journey of understanding yourself.

feedback

You may also be able to arrange some feedback from those around you. This can range from merely asking a handful of people who know how you work to give you some evidence-based feedback, to undertaking a full 360 degree feedback process (this is described in Chapter 12, but essentially is a way of getting structured feedback from a variety of sources split into categories – say, your boss, direct reports, peers, customers, etc)[5].

5 It's important to remember that any form of feedback is about perception, which may or may not reflect reality. It's still useful data, however – you can change how people perceive you if you are aware of the impact you are having on them. Try not to get defensive ('How dare you'), judgmental ('Well, he would say that, wouldn't he?') or make excuses. Just accept it as data; what you choose to do with it is up to you.

chapter 6

development options

Now we've looked at the *why*, *what* and *how* of personal development, let's turn our attention to progressing it: your development options.

It's amazing how many of us, when deciding on how to address our development needs, automatically default to booking ourselves on a training course. Not that there's anything wrong with training courses, but my point is that there are many different ways to address a development need. If you think creatively about other development options[1] you can often save the training budget for targeted training interventions.

Consider these alternative options:

- **Project work**: Can you get assigned on a project which will not only tap into an area of expertise but also stretch you? You can try taking a different role from your usual one, and when reviewing the project consider both the end result

1 This section is focused on you, but the same principles apply when having development conversations with your staff, of course. More in Section four ...

(content) and how you all got there – as well as what you learnt about yourself and group work (process).

- **Temporary secondment/job swap**: Some organisations have extensive schemes relating to this. The benefits are large (cross-boundary awareness and networking, organisational understanding) but the costs organisationally can be high if done properly. Again, make the learning explicit by doing a thorough review of content and process.
- **Coaching**: As we'll discuss in Chapter 13, both being coached and being a coach are learning interventions for both parties. Coaching in a group setting – often referred to as *action learning sets* – can be of enormous benefit for all concerned (I often incorporate them as a key learning intervention into management development programmes).
- **Reading, watching films and documentaries**: Being part of (or setting up) an informal work-focused book club, where ideas relating to the book are discussed, can be both fun and informative – and can form the basis of the action learning sets mentioned above.
- **Presenting**: Presenting to others about a topic improves and works on your (transferable) presentation and public speaking skills, while in-depth learning on a subject you previously knew little about may get the creative juices flowing. And we teach best what we most need to learn.

understanding your learning style

Not all options appeal equally to everyone. Understanding your own learning style influences how you take in information and what you are naturally drawn to. Some people prefer to read, for example, while others prefer the face-to-face contact of a training course or discussion group.

learning styles model

Peter Honey and Alan Mumford[2] developed a useful model of learning styles in the 1970s that has been used extensively in the business community. This model has two components; an evolution of an earlier experiential model (Kolb's learning model) of a learning intervention, and the styles that individuals are typically drawn to. The stages of an effective learning intervention are:

---

2 *Manual of Learning Styles* (1982). You can complete the associated questionnaire online at www.peterhoney.com for a small charge.

- having a learning experience
- reviewing that experience
- drawing conclusions from it
- planning consequences or next steps.

Try to get into the habit of following this model whenever you undertake a learning intervention. If nothing else, it makes filling in your next appraisal documentation so much easier!

According to Honey and Mumford, our learning preferences have an often hidden but powerful impact on what we learn and the way we do it. Understanding your own learning preferences can help you choose learning interventions that are more targeted to you; although there's also something to be said for going outside your comfort zone and trying out the other styles occasionally – to expand your bandwidth, as Peter Honey puts it. These typical learning styles are:

- **Activist**: people who like to involve themselves fully in new experiences and being happy to just do it! They enjoy the challenge of being thrown in at the deep end and will often think about the consequences later. They often learn through trial and error. Activists would learn best through chairing meetings and doing presentations, role-playing and trying things out for themselves; they may not be drawn to lecture-based material or reading.
- **Reflector**: people who like to be told what to do and be thoroughly briefed before trying it out for themselves. They like to analyse methodically, collecting data and thinking things through before coming to conclusions. Reflectors learn best through being 'taught'; they are unlikely to warm to activity-based learning or role-play situations.
- **Theorist**: people who like complex theories about why things work, preferring a clear purpose and interesting, challenging goals. They like to be intellectually stimulated and may require some convincing before accepting the learning. They prefer a logical, consistent approach and don't respond well to poorly-briefed activities or some experiential, emotional interventions, being uncomfortable with subjectivity.
- **Pragmatist**: people who like to observe and watch demonstrations about how something is done before trying it themselves. They are practical, down-to-earth and want a clear link between the learning intervention and what they can actually do with it in the real world. They are usually happy to try things out for themselves but want clear guidelines or a practice run first.

neuro linguistic programming

Another model often used is taken from the world of neuro linguistic programming (NLP). This is a body of theoretical and practical work that is primarily concerned with the link between our behaviour and our representations of the world – how we think and feel.

Representational Systems is an NLP model that is concerned with our processing of information, and suggests that we have a preference for the sort of information we primarily attend to. There are five senses, three of which tend to become sensory-based preferences; we use all three but it's likely that one or two will dominate and become our mental strategy for dealing with data:

- Some people have a **visual** preference; they store memories as pictures, usually have good spatial awareness and use a lot of visual words (*I see what you mean, let me paint you a picture,* etc). Some believe that visual people commonly look up and to the right when imagining images, and up and to the left when remembering images[3].
- Other people have an **auditory** preference; instead of images they store sounds or dialogue, and use auditory words (*I hear what you're saying, that resonates with me*). They look on the level and to the right when imagining and the left when recalling data.
- Finally, some people have a **kinaesthetic** preference; they store sensations and emotions and use associated words (*I feel that you're right, I'm in touch with what you're saying*). They tend to look down and to the right when imagining, and down and to the left when recalling.

Of course we use all of these at various points, and they are unlikely to be in our conscious awareness. It also doesn't particularly matter which one or ones is/are your preference(s). Understanding the model and seeing what makes sense (I've just given away my own visual preference) means you may be able to tailor your learning activities accordingly.

your development plan

So we've looked at the *why* of development, the *what* and now some ideas as to the *how*. Use this information and understanding to start thinking of your own

3 Apparently, enough salespeople believe in this that it's often used in sales training.

development plan; when you've finished this book you may wish to add to it (and certainly use it as part of your managerial learning log).

role-modelling

I mentioned in the Introduction that I've learned a lot from other managers – both good and bad. After reading this book, you may wish to choose a role model you admire from whom you can learn. Ask yourself:

- What qualities do they have?
- What are their belief systems?
- What are their motivational drivers?
- What would they do in this situation?
- What aspects of them can you borrow?

There's nothing that any manager of people can do that you can't. It may just take a bit of knowledge and then meaningful, focused practice so it becomes locked into your basal ganglia – the part of the brain that's automatic and beyond conscious awareness; where we have 'unconscious competence'.

This focused, conscious practice concept is important and is what makes the difference between 'length of time in post' and 'growing in the job'. If we don't actively engage our practice muscles, get out of our comfort zone, forget our limiting beliefs, and review specifically and systematically what we've learnt, we just stand still. Make these opportunities happen!

practice

Many of the skills of performance- and development-based conversations described in this book will help you get optimum performance out of your team. And such skills can be applied to yourself and your own development just as effectively.

It may take 10,000 hours of conscious, focused practice over ten years to become world class[4], but no-one's asking for perfection. Good will do, and you can do this in a matter of months. Besides, you probably have at least 20 years' experience in having these conversations already.

4 According to Matthew Syed (*Bounce: The Myth of Talent and the Power of Practice*) and Malcolm Gladwell (*Outliers: The Story of Success*).

section checklist

the psychological manager:

- Has the attitude that people management is a fundamental part of the job and reflects this attitude in the amount of time and effort spent doing it.
- Accepts that their own development managerially is just as important as their team's, and accepts that being seen to be doing this is role-modelling great behaviour.
- Thinks about their own skills portfolio and what needs to be added to get them to where they want to be.
- Is able to deal flexibly with change and uncertainty, acknowledging that collaboration, innovation and dealing with ambiguity are increasingly important skills to have.
- Is prepared to let go of elements of the day job to allow their team to develop through delegation and then is prepared to spend time coaching them.
- Is in touch with their own value systems, motivations and beliefs, and is aware of the impact these have on future direction.
- Is aware of their own strengths and weaknesses, how they learn and their typical interpersonal styles – and actively seeks feedback on these areas.
- Understands the theory and practice of emotional intelligence; recognises and controls their own emotions and recognises and deals appropriately with the emotions of others to achieve a desired outcome.
- Recognises that emotions are contagious, and a manager's emotions especially so.
- Creatively expands the definition of a development intervention to go beyond training. This may include project work, stretch assignments, secondments, coaching, becoming a coach, reading and presenting to others – reviewing all learning interventions accordingly.

section
three

we are all the same.
but different

• 7 • intelligence • 8 • personality • 9 • beliefs, attitudes and knowledge • 10 • motivation • section checklist: the psychological manager •

understanding individual differences

Up to now the attention has been on you, since you can't expect your team to focus on high performance and development if you're not role-modelling these behaviours yourself (if only to avoid accusations of hypocrisy!).

Now we look at the factors that make us all different from each other. In addition to the (usually) obvious ways in which people differ – such as age, gender, race and culture, for example[1] – we also all vary in some key psychological constructs that are less immediately discernible[2].

The full list of these variables is probably infinite, but psychologists tend to collapse them into the four following categories:

- intelligence
- personality
- beliefs, attitudes and knowledge
- motivation.

A brief overview of these categories is useful for the simple reason that with some of them, at least, you as a manager can have a real impact.

An individual's *skill* to perform a task is a function of their intelligence, personality preferences and their beliefs, attitudes and knowledge/experience; what determines their *will* is their motivation (with a dose of attitude thrown in).

Once you understand these key psychological constructs, you – as a Psychological Manager – can use this information to better understand the individual members of your team.

---

1 Which usually have nothing to do with variations in job performance ...

2 Which do.

chapter 7

intelligence

The first psychological construct we look at is intelligence; and there's pretty much nothing you can do about this one. Intelligence is usually thought of as our capacity for logic and abstract thought, understanding, reasoning and problem solving; however, if you got 50 psychologists together in a room[1] you'd get at least that many definitions – and probably more[2].

attempts to measure intelligence

The measurement of intelligence as a scientific pursuit started with Charles Darwin's cousin, Francis Galton; he measured reaction times to thinking tasks, which was fair enough, and measured people's heads, which wasn't. Many early theories (Spearman, Burt and Vernon among others) agreed with the premise of a general factor of intelligence that affected most areas of functioning (called *g*), whereas others suggested there was less of a correlation between all the

1 Don't try this at home.

2 As some like to argue with themselves.

components, which included verbal and numerical reasoning, memory, spatial ability and inductive reasoning (Thurstone's *Primary Mental Abilities*, 1938).

Later theories, helped by advances in neuroscience, have tended to stress the complexity of multiple intelligences that are largely independent of each other, while reacting together when required. Howard Gardner (1983) posited the existence of seven intelligences; linguistic, logical-mathematical, spatial, musical, bodily kinaesthetic, interpersonal and intrapersonal. Gardner is often credited with opening the door to the emotional intelligence concepts described in Chapter 4.

IQ testing

Most of the last 100 years or so of research into the world of intelligence has been focused on its measurement, leading to the widely used concept of Intelligence Quotient (IQ), measured through psychometric testing. This is not without its critics, with many asserting that IQ tests measure what IQ tests measure (which may or may not be the same as intelligence), but the concept has certainly stuck.

All IQ tests are standardised during design to provide a normal distribution (the bell-shaped curve) with a mean of 100. This means, therefore, that 50% of a population will have an IQ of less than this; 50% an IQ of more. Psychometric tests conform to a set of standards of reliability (consistency over time and internally within the questions themselves) and validity (whether they measure what they say they measure).

IQ tends to be an amalgam of verbal, numerical and abstract reasoning, together with spatial awareness – the much maligned 11+ in the British schooling system was/is effectively an IQ test. In the workplace, however, any measurement tends to be split out to reflect the requirements of the job. Tests are widely used for recruitment and selection purposes (numerical reasoning tests for accountancy jobs, for example) but rather less for development reasons. The reason for this is somewhat contentious (to grossly underestimate the depth of feeling on this issue) – whether intelligence is innate and inherited, or a result of experiences and environment after conception. The argument has an impact on development, because if we accept that intelligence is largely a result of our genetic inheritance then there's not much we can do to develop it.

nature/nurture

The pendulum between nature and nurture has swung pretty consistently over the last 100 years, often aided by the use of studies into identical twins who've been brought up apart. This has also been reflected politically, with some writers arguing that the political right leans more towards nature[3] and the left is more inclined towards nurture[4].

This pendulum has gone pretty much from 80:20 to 20:80, and somewhat conveniently the heritability factor now seems to be stuck in the middle. Moreover, many argue that it's the interaction between the two that's actually the point.

environmental factors

However the heritability cake is divided, environmental factors have an influence on our intelligence, at least up until puberty. These factors include levels of individual attention and encouragement from parents and/or significant others, general family atmosphere, resources such as books and even diet; in an article published by the *Journal of Epidemiology and Community Health* in 2011, Kate Northstone argued that when confounding variables were taken out of the equation, a diet rich in processed foods at the age of three was associated with a correspondingly lower IQ at the age of eight; for every (positive) point of increase on the dietary pattern score, there was a 1.2 point increase in IQ.

fixed intelligence

What most researchers tend to agree on is that by puberty, our intelligence in the stricter definitions of the term tends to be pretty fixed, perhaps going down a tad after 35 or so. It's useful to think of this as the hardware – we can choose to run more up-to-date software on it but the essential physical computer is always there.

So as a manager there's not much you can do to help your staff develop their basic IQ (although with concerted practice we can certainly get better at using what we've got). As far as building skill goes, you're far better off concentrating on the other dimensions of individual differences to enable the more 'fixed' intelligence of your staff to be used at its optimum.

---

3 'So let's use this IQ test to identify who goes to grammar school so they are not held back by the undevelopable' (I may be taking some artistic licence here ...)

4 'Let's put everyone together and stream them so they can move upstream if they work hard and downstream if they don't ...'

chapter 8

personality

The second psychological construct is personality. This has also kept a lot of psychologists very busy for many years, and for those of us who prefer certainty and clarity over ambiguity and open-endedness (itself a personality characteristic – see the Myers Briggs Personality Indicator © in Chapter 19) the plethora of models and theories can be very frustrating. A few of them are detailed here for your interest, but most of them are not of much practical use to the average manager until we get to the psychometric approach.

One distinction to draw, however, is between *idiographic* and *nomothetic* approaches, as they conveniently divide the plethora of theories into these two categories:

- **Idiographic** theories are based on what makes us different from everyone else: the sum total of our experiences and background (including genetic makeup) that makes us unique. To look at these we'll revisit a few paradigms, or schools of thought, from Chapter 2: psychoanalytic, behaviourist, cognitive and humanist.

- **Nomothetic** approaches are more concerned with identifying the dimensions of personality that we all have, but in which we vary in terms of amount. These approaches led to the world of psychometric testing, used widely in organisations for selection, development and teambuilding purposes.

First of all, though, a somewhat obvious myth-buster. We don't have 'a lot of personality' or 'no personality' as such (these are often simplistic and judgemental evaluations of extraversion/introversion). Instead, we vary in our personal and interpersonal style along certain dimensions (in most theories, *types* or *traits*) when compared to others.

idiographic personality theories

In Chapter 2 we explored the various paradigms that psychology has gone through since its inception as a science. The history of personality theory and research is part of the same play, with many of the same actors involved. For example, if we ignore Hippocrates' four humours (our illnesses and personality characteristics are created by an imbalance of four substances – blood, yellow bile, black bile and phlegm (so an excess of phlegm makes us phlegmatic)), which seemed to be the predominant theory for at least 2,500 years, then it pretty much starts with Freud and the psychoanalytic school.

Freudian theory

A full explanation of how Freud claimed our personalities develop is beyond the scope of this book[1], but many readers will be aware of the stages of development he suggested children go through on their way to adulthood (oral, anal, phallic, latency and genital) and how we can get fixated at any of these stages if we fail to overcome the problems associated with them. Fixation causes us to hang on to some of the characteristics of the particular stage – for example, a fixation at the oral stage may result in smoking or gluttony.

Freud also posited a structure of the personality. Each of the three components has its own function, and when working healthily has a system of checks and balances to produce well-balanced, adult behaviour[2]. The psychological constructs (not physical entities) are as follows:

---

1 Or perhaps I'm just repressing it. Second Freudian joke.

2 These concepts can be used practically in conversations using the Transactional Analysis model of parent, adult, child.

- The **id**: primitive, irrational and instinctual and operates according to the pleasure principle in that it is motivated to seek pleasure and avoid the tension of psychological pain. It is free from any inhibitions and does not recognise such concepts as fear or anxiety. This is our inner child, and once we learn as a child that we need to delay gratification (see page 35), as there's an external world out there that we need to adapt to, the next construct develops ...
- The **ego**: the part that operates according to the reality principle in that it takes account of the real world's constraints. It tries to satisfy the demands of the id but in an appropriate, adult way. To do this it has to learn cognitive strategies, such as thinking, learning, deciding and memorising.
- The **superego**: this develops later (Freud argued at around age five) and constitutes our sense of right and wrong – a sort of conscience – derived from our increasing socialisation and understanding of the rules and norms of society, and is greatly affected by our experience of parenting and culture. It is said to be fully developed when we replace parental control with self control.

These three parts of our personality are continually in conflict, and when these conflicts are unresolved they find expression through our dreams, neurotic symptoms such as anxiety attacks and irrational fears, or physical symptoms such as paralysis. To try to mitigate the effects of these and other anxieties we develop defence mechanisms, many of which have transferred to common parlance.

Short-term use of these defences is healthy; but it's not psychologically healthy to rely on them constantly or for long periods. Examples are repression, denial and projection; these are now widely regarded as 'truisms', as we see them every day. For example, repression and denial are accepted parts of the change curve; with projection we notice in others what we don't like to admit to in ourselves, so we 'project' those characteristics or feelings on to others.

With the exception of understanding and learning to notice these defence mechanisms, most applications of Freudian theory tend to belong in the world of therapy, rather than management or coaching. The psychodynamic approach tends to involve going back to the past (usually childhood) to help address problems in the present, and the role of unconscious desires and forces that may be having an impact on behaviour[3].

---

3 Just don't go there, basically.

Carl Jung and the psyche

A certain post-Freudian has, however, found favour with the business world. Carl Jung, a former Freudian disciple[4], took psychoanalytic theory in a new direction, calling the personality the *psyche* and viewing it as made up of our consciousness, our personal unconscious and the collective unconscious (its contents being ancestral and racial memories handed down through heredity and known as archetypes[5]). The part of the mind that we are aware of is the consciousness, and how we experience the world through this consciousness is the backbone of the MBTI[6]. This is described in Chapter 19; it's now probably the world's most popular personality questionnaire and is used extensively in coaching and teambuilding. It is a type approach, as opposed to a trait approach.

The common theme with the psychoanalytic models is that much of what shapes our personalities and subsequent behaviour is unknown to us and deeply rooted in childhood experience. As such, with the exception of the MBTI © and the Tavistock Institute, which specialises in this school of thought, their transferability to the workplace is limited.

I did, however, come across one organisation in Australia that used the Rorschach Test as part of its selection methodology. This is the famous 'inkblot' test and is known as a projective test because the participant 'projects' their descriptions of and responses to an ambiguous shape. Interpretation is highly skilled, arguably subjective and unreliable, and while there's limited evidence for it in a clinical setting, using it as part of your recruitment and selection strategy is not recommended[7].

learned behaviour

At the same time as Freud was developing his theories of personality, behaviourists such as John Watson and B.F. Skinner were taking a more scientific approach. They felt that the introspective theorising of Freud et al was too subjective and untestable, and therefore had little value in the new 'science' of psychology. The central claim, influenced at least initially by the pioneering work of Pavlov at the turn of the century, was that much of our behaviour is learned; we start from a *tabula rasa*, or blank slate, and through learning we acquire our knowledge, attitudes, insights and personality.

---

4 'Sigmund, old fellow – not everything is about sex, you know ...'

5 Such as God, characters in fairy stories, the Hero, etc.

6 The Myers Briggs Type Indicator ©.

7 And in any event would only tell you things you didn't want to know.

Pavlov discovered that if you presented an unconnected stimulus to a dog – such as the ringing of a bell – at the same time as food then eventually the dog would start salivating at the sound of the bell alone. The bell had become a conditioned stimulus; the new relationship became known as a *conditioned reflex* and the process was called *classical conditioning*.

Watson argued that we learned through a process called *positive reinforcement*. We respond to a particular stimulus, and if there are positive consequences resulting from our response we do it again. If the outcome is not so favourable, we don't – or at least adjust our behaviour accordingly.

Watson took Pavlov's concept of classical conditioning and applied it in a well-known case[8] to a one-year-old child. Albert showed no fear of rats before the experiment; after being subjected to frightening loud noises at the same time as being shown a tame rat, he then displayed all the classic fear responses when shown the rat without the noise. He then generalised this fear to all things with fur, such as coats – and even Watson's hair. It took only seven times.

Watson's work was expanded on and refined by Skinner, who became one of the most influential psychologists of the twentieth century. To Skinner, the very concept of free will was almost unthinkable; our behaviour is completely determined by the history of our conditioning experiences. There is no 'inner self' that freely chooses how to respond to stimuli. We react to events in predictable ways – in ways no different from the rats and pigeons he used in his experiments[9].

Any talk of values or concepts of good or bad is really concerned with the positive or negative reinforcing effects of stimuli, nothing more. Things are good only if they ultimately aid survival, because we have learned that this is so. In Chapter 14 on will and motivation, I draw a parallel with the 'carrot and stick' approach to management – again, positive or negative reinforcers as ways to shape behaviour. To the behaviourists, what's actually going on in people's heads is unknowable and largely irrelevant – or at least not fit for study.

cognitive theory

The cognitive school took a very different approach. They argued that the basic *stimulus » response* premise was too simplistic, and that learning does not take place in such a vacuum. Information is perceived, evaluated and decisions made on the basis of it with the additional context of prior knowledge and beliefs.

8 'Little Albert' (1920). Because of those pesky ethics people, you'd never get away with this today.

9 Many readers will have heard of the 'Skinner box' where semi-starved animals are conditioned to press levers to get food; at first by accident, then by learning through repetition and reinforcement.

Logic and rationality are at the heart of many of the cognitive theories, and the questioning and challenging of beliefs, thought processes and perceptions are at the heart of many associated therapeutic models[10].

personal constructs

One of the most important of these theories was developed by George Kelly. His take on personality is that we are all natural thinkers – scientists, even – attempting to understand the world we live in by interpreting it according to our unique hypotheses and understandings. These hypotheses are continually tested and amended as necessary, and our actions subsequently derive from them. They build up into a way of looking at the world – what Kelly called a *personal construct*.

We are not passive reactors to stimuli, according to Kelly. We are active in building our own individual concept of reality – a philosophical position known as *constructive alternativism*[11]. Our realities are personal, idiosyncratic and based on our interpretation of our experiences in the world. Our personality, then, is this unique personal construct system. There is more free will here – we can choose to review and alter our constructs – but only if we're aware of them. Kelly's therapeutic approach was based on enabling people to become aware of their personal constructs through a method known as the repertory grid.

To understand someone's personality therefore is to understand their personal constructs. These are like lenses through which we view the world, putting a particular spin on that world depending on what lenses we are using. These constructs are often depicted as opposing (to the individual) pairs, such as intelligent vs stupid, friendly vs hostile, affluent vs poor, truth vs Government[12]. They enable us to impose order and predictability on to the world; living without these filters would be chaotic as we'd be awash with both data and a sense of unpredictability. Our own individual construct system determines what we pay attention to, our beliefs and value systems and ultimately our behaviour.

The repertory grid was originally devised to determine an individual's personal constructs. After selecting a group of roles (significant others such as friends, colleagues, people you admire, yourself) the individual is asked to select three at random and determine in what way two of them are similar to each other but different from the third. By continually repeating the process,

10 Such as Rational-Emotive Therapy and Cognitive Behavioural Therapy (CBT – the sort you tend to get on the NHS).

11 Aristotle said that 'A is A' (only in Greek). But constructive alternativism would say that 'A is what we construe, or construct, as A'.

12 OK, I made this last one up.

a pattern of constructs emerges. This technique has been borrowed by organisations as a market research tool, in determining training needs and in performing job analyses.

humanist theories

Finally, no trawl through personality theory is complete without mentioning the humanist approaches. Two names stand out: Abraham Maslow, whose hierarchy of needs is considered in Chapter 10, and Carl Rogers and his 'Self' theory.

It's hard not to get a bit depressed when reviewing the history of personality theories. We start off with everything being hidden and a product of basic urges (Freud), through being a stimulus/response machine with no more personality than a rat in a Skinner box[13] and at last, with the cognitive theories, a thinking – if not always knowing – or emotional creature. With the humanist schools of thought, and most particularly the work of Rogers, the 'human' comes back into being, erm, human.

Carl Rogers

Rogers was a phenomenologist. He believed that all of us live in our own changing, subjective world that includes our experiences, emotions and beliefs about ourselves and the world. This is our reality; no more or less valid than anyone else's, but unique to us, and a portion of this reality defines the concept of *I* or *me*. Rogers called this the *perceived self*, and it has an impact on how we behave in the world. The only way of understanding another person's subjective view of the world (and the resulting behaviours) is to get into their frame of reference; the ultimate goal of therapy and the result of a truly empathic relationship. Rogers believed that a way of achieving empathy is to demonstrate unconditional positive regard, thereby fulfilling a basic human need.

This is the acceptance of an individual's worth without judgement; what a child craves from its parents[14]. Rogers believed that many psychological disorders are created when we attempt to gain positive regard from others by living our lives the way those others want us to. This perceived self (the *I* we believe ourselves to be) can be contrasted with the ideal self – our perception of who we would like (or ought) to be. Psychological health occurs when our perceived self and our ideal self are congruent (either the same or compatible); in other words, we are giving ourselves unconditional positive regard.

13 Perhaps not the most unbiased sentence I've ever written.

14 Parents who say 'I'll love you *if* you tidy your room' are not demonstrating unconditional positive regard.

When we look at Maslow's hierarchy of needs in Chapter 10, you'll notice that the ultimate motivating force is the need for self actualisation; the process of being who we are most capable of being. This positive, humanistic concept is also at the core of Rogers' theory. We are born with an actualising tendency; to become a fully functioning individual with a drive towards psychological and physical health (he called it living the good life) to reach our full potential. Where Rogers differs from Maslow is that Maslow posited a hierarchy, with self actualisation at the top (passing through physical and social needs along the way), whereas Rogers suggests that this is the only motivating force; everything else is part of this ultimate aim of optimal development. A fully functioning person:

- is open to experience
- lives fully in each and every moment
- does what feels right
- is free to live their life in the way they see fit
- is naturally creative.

Unlike Freud, Rogers did not accept that behaviour is necessarily a result of past events. He preferred to think of it as a 'here and now' response to our perception of the reality of the world around us. He did, however, agree with Freud's concept of the defence mechanism, at least in that we can use denial processes by refusing to recognise anything that threatens our self concept, and selectively distort or rationalise perceptions until they have a better fit with our self concept.

The main applications of Rogers' work are in education[15] and therapy, although many coaches and facilitators borrow heavily from the rapport building, empathic and person-centered approach to interventions.

nomothetic personality theories

So far we've looked at some key idiographic theories of personality. Our experiences have made us unique, and we can only understand and predict the complexities of human behaviour one person at a time. As far as the workplace

15 The Robin Williams' film *Dead Poets Society* has many Rogerian references and themes in that as a new teacher in a traditional school he tries to get away from the jug-and-mug approach of pouring knowledge into empty vessels, and instead teaches them how to free their minds in a 'fully functioning' way. Doesn't end particularly well, now I come to think about it.

is concerned, this is great if you have a department therapist, but in the real world this is not usually an option.

The nomothetic approach is arguably more scientific, in that nomothetic theories are more concerned with dimensions of personality that we all have to a greater or lesser extent; these approaches therefore have the sheer weight of numbers on their side. They also allow us to compare individuals against set criteria (and each other). For this reason they have resulted in the world of psychometric profiling; an approach used extensively in recruitment and selection as well as training, development and teambuilding.

traits

The nomothetic approach tends to make use of the concept of traits when referring to dimensions of personality. Traits are those aspects of personality that we all have, to a greater or lesser extent. When psychometric tests are designed along the theoretical frameworks laid down by the great trait theorists (Eysenck, Cattell), they are structured so that each trait is normally distributed along the classic bell curve; individuals assessing themselves through these questionnaires are compared to a large sample of people who have taken the test before (a norm group) and so will see where they stand on the normal distribution curve.

An example would be the trait Dominance; at the right-hand side of the bell curve we have the Dominant end and at the left we have the Submissive end, with most people being in the middle. Your score determines where on that curve you see yourself compared to the norm group (usually general population, UK managers and professionals, or graduates).

The main difference between trait approaches and the idiographic theories we've examined above is that the latter tend not to have a particular theoretical base to then try to 'prove' during clinical and experimental research. In this sense the former trait approaches are effectively data-driven approaches, as opposed to theory driven. This is usually performed through the statistical technique known as factor analysis[16].

A trait, then, is generally thought of as a relatively stable pattern of behaviour

---

16 This is a bit like putting a load of data into a centrifuge, spinning it and seeing what lumps or clusters come out. It's a way of statistically uncovering any hidden structure or relationships (correlations) behind the data. These clusters end up being labelled as traits. No theory is involved; what comes out of the analysis determines the trait model, and it can be carved up in many different ways.

or other aspect of personality. Gordon Allport, one of the original protagonists of this approach, called them dispositions[17]. While the principles behind the various trait theories remain the same, arguably the main contentious issue is the number of traits that adequately describe human behaviour.

Eysenck's three personality traits

Hans Eysenck contended that the number of personality traits could be reduced to three: extraversion, neuroticism and psychoticism. The extravert/introvert distinction was previously identified by Jung, but where Jung talked about it in terms of whether we are getting our energy from the external world or internal resources[18], Eysenck referred more to sociability, risk taking and impulsiveness (Extravert) or quiet, serious, restrained and reserved (Introvert).

Neuroticism was about emotional stability (or not), suggesting that neurotic individuals were typically anxious, irritable and worrying; highly stable individuals, however, were calm, controlled and more restrained in their emotional responses.

Psychoticism was added later, and referred to the tendency towards lacking empathy, being insensitive or even hostile. This last trait, Eysenck argued, was not normally distributed like the other two; in other words, most people are at the non-psychotic end of the normal distribution curve[19].

Eysenck contended that there were biological and genetic components to personality[20]; to him, extraversion was primarily caused by reduced baseline cortical arousal levels (so extraverted individuals are continually seeking stimulation, whereas introverts have quite enough of it already), and neuroticism was largely hereditary.

Questionnaires based on Eysenck's work[21] tend to be used more for research purposes than occupational ones, but he does remain one of the most cited theorists in the history of psychology. He was in almost constant battle with our next trait theorist, Raymond Cattell, over the number of traits that personality can be usefully broken down to, but their similarities vastly outweigh their differences. It just depends on how you cut the personality cake.

---

17 He is also responsible for the concept of the idiographic/nomothetic distinction.

18 See page 168 on the MBTI ©.

19 Although you may be unsurprised to know that there appears to be an over-representation of high psychoticism scores within the prison population (see page 36, footnote 7 on the BBC *Horizon* programme of September 2011).

20 He had rather robust views on the variations of IQ scores of various races, too.

21 The Eysenck Personality Inventory (EPI) and Eysenck Personality Questionnaire (EPQ).

Cattell's 16 personality factors

Cattell's great drive was to make psychology (and the study of intelligence and personality in particular) a real science, breaking away from the verbal theorising of Freud et al; if something exists, it can be measured. Cattell was instrumental in developing the factor analysis techniques described above, and through his research developed a multi-level model of personality traits that has stood the test of time (and of tests – his model is often used as the starting point for personality questionnaires).

Through his analysis (using everyday life behaviours, data from experimental situations and questionnaire data) Cattell came up with 16 fundamental factors (he called them primary factors) underlying human personality, each with its own associated set of behaviours. These factors remain relatively stable over time, although they can be temporarily affected by mood state. He named them after the letters of the alphabet to avoid any preconceptions associated with existing terms, and developed one of the world's most widely used personality questionnaires – the 16PF™ – to measure them. This questionnaire is used for a variety of purposes: selection, development, coaching and counselling and in clinical settings[22].

On the 16PF, each trait or factor is normally distributed (an individual's score can be mapped on to the bell-shaped curve) with separate descriptions for left-hand and right-hand positions, and with most of the population falling in the middle. Examples are:

- Factor A: **Warmth**, with the left-hand position referring to a tendency to be reserved, cool and detached, and the right-hand position as outgoing and warmhearted.
- Factor C: **Emotional Stability**, with the left-hand position referring to emotional instability and being easily upset, and the right-hand as more emotionally stable, calm and mature.

An individual's scores on each of the 16 factors (and also occupational groups such as solicitors, IT workers and nurses) can therefore be visually represented as a profile for ease of interpretation. This approach is also

22 My first proper job as an occupational psychologist was with the 16PF™ publishers for the UK version of the questionnaire, and I spent my four years there training people to be qualified to use it. Somewhat coincidentally (I assume) Cattell died on the day I joined.

used by subsequent questionnaires such as SHL's Occupational Personality Questionnaire (the OPQ32r[23]); again, widely used in industry for both selection and development purposes.

When Cattell factor-analysed these 16 factors, he found that they could be collapsed down to five second-order – or global – factors; each one of these five was made up of four or five primary factors that tended to go together in the real world. As an example, an individual's score on the global factor **Extraversion** is made up of their scores on five primary factors: Warmth, Vigilance, Social Boldness, Privateness and Self-reliance. If each of these scores is high, the result will be a high score on Extraversion.

Big Five global factors: OCEAN

These five global factors are important. The vast majority of research and cross-validation with other personality questionnaires suggests that personality has these five overarching domains, now known in personality theory as the Big Five. This is heartening for the practitioner; we can be as confident as we can be that we are using a model that is empirically driven from a variety of sources[24]. These Big Five are known by the acronym OCEAN:

- **Openness**: appreciation for variety, creativity, culture, independence.
- **Conscientiousness**: self discipline, responsibility, planned rather than spontaneous.
- **Extraversion**: outgoing, energetic, seeks company, sociable.
- **Agreeableness**: good-natured, friendly and compassionate, co-operative.
- **Neuroticism**: sensitive, nervous, experiences strong emotions, less emotionally stable.

You'll notice that both Cattell's and Eysenck's work are reflected here. As mentioned, the 16PF and EPQ measure all or some of the Big Five; the OPQ32r can give an assessment of them, and the NEO Personality Inventory can give a specific measure of them[25]. All five factors are said to derive from both nature and nurture, all conveniently approximating a 50:50 split.

23 Guess how many traits this one measures ...

24 'The "Big Five" has become a widely accepted template for understanding the structure of human personality'; Arnold and Randall et al, page 116.

25 Costa and McCrae (1985).

using theories in practice

So there we have it: a brief and definitely not exhaustive look at the world of personality theory.

But of course when we have our performance- or development-based conversations with our staff, we don't usually have these personality models in our head to aid us. Instead we use our implicit theories; our own subjective assumptions and stereotypes about how people are and how they work (and, as we shall see in Chapter 10, on what motivates them).

In essence, we take cognitive shortcuts and give them labels – an approach not dissimilar to the trait approach but with one major difference – they do not involve any semblance of science or objectivity. They are made up of our attitudes, social and cultural beliefs and our life experiences; as such, we're often wrong, or at least biased. Our implicit beliefs affect what we notice; we selectively attend and distort, which has the result of reinforcing our beliefs.

Social psychologists call this the *fundamental attribution error*. We place greater emphasis on (madeup) personality variables when looking for explanations of human behaviour than on situational variables[26]. It takes greater effort to consider all the possible situational scenarios that may have had an impact on people's behaviour, so instead we put it down to being something about *them*. Add to this our own emotional state at the time and our preference for consistency when categorising people and events, and we have a pretty good recipe for getting it wrong.

Managers can't be expected to be experts in personality theory, so avoiding the automatic stereotyping of people and behaviours has to be a good move. As we'll see in Section four, taking a coaching approach to these conversations helps us to take a step back from wading in with our own, often flawed, perspectives.

This isn't to say that personality is an irrelevance to the manager. Having an awareness of the dimensions of Jungian typology via the MBTI © is a path many managers follow during teambuilding events, which can also add value to one-to-one conversations. Many organisations use the concept of traits – psychometric profiling – during the recruitment and selection stage and use this to inform their subsequent conversations and management style.

---

26 Though we tend to do the opposite with our own behaviour.

It's important, however, to remember that all such methods and tools are best used as the starting point for conversations and need to be fully understood by the parties concerned – most of them require rigorous training before use and as such, this work is often carried out either by external consultants or internal experts within HR or recruitment departments.

chapter 9

beliefs, attitudes and knowledge

This third area of individual differences, often grouped together in the field of *epistemology*, are related but distinct concepts. Beliefs are often thought of as more of a philosophical concept, but psychologists have also had a lot to say on the matter, especially when it comes to the effect belief has on behaviour.

beliefs

It sounds obvious, but most of our beliefs come from our upbringing. We internalise the culture around us – which includes religion, social class, educational opportunities and circumstances, parental values and the like. Many of us cling to these without question, but as Rogers would argue (see Chapter 8), fully functioning individuals are continually questioning and searching for 'truth'.

The world of neuro linguistic programming[1] also has a lot to say about beliefs. To NLP practitioners, beliefs are the determinants of success or failure. We can choose to believe something that will help us, and we choose (although we may not be aware of that choosing process) to be bound negatively by them. To quote Richard Bach, 'Argue for your limitations, and sure enough, they're yours'[2]. Just as our staff have beliefs about work, or themselves, or their profession that help or hinder them, so do we as managers – but we may also have beliefs about them too.

A useful belief to hold is one of 'people are separate from their behaviours' – similar to the old adage 'love the sinner, hate the sin'. In this way we avoid stereotyping and demonising people, and can help them work on and change any errant behaviour as opposed to trying to change them as a person – an ultimately futile task.

Through powerful coaching-style conversations, we can help people change their thinking about tasks, which should lead to different results, or reinforce any behaviour we wish them to maintain. This may be about confidence-boosting; the Psychological Manager takes pastoral duties seriously! Our beliefs about ourselves can affect the little voice we all have in our heads. Negative self talk can have a huge impact on our confidence and a huge impact on performance. It's a vicious circle:

negative beliefs » negative thoughts » negative behaviours » negative outcomes » reinforce negative beliefs » ad infinitum ...

Another classic belief dimension – and one that leaks into personality theory – is the *locus of control* theory of Julian Rotter. This describes the extent to which we believe that we control events, or that they control us.

Those with a high internal locus of control have the belief that events arise from their own actions as opposed to fate or the actions of others. This affects their behaviour in that they tend to influence others more readily, tend to assume they will be successful, and generally feel more able to own that success rather than put it down to chance. Rotter felt that the internal/external locus of control

1 The dark art of NLP; used a lot in sales and some coaching interventions. Essentially it is a suite of tools and techniques focused on the link between emotions, thoughts and behaviour. It comes with a set of beliefs that practitioners should subscribe to – one of which being 'A person's behaviour is not the person'.

2 Richard Bach's *Illusions* – a catalyst when I needed one when going from being a rubbish banker to a hopefully less rubbish student of psychology.

was a continuum (more like a trait) than a bipolar type – with the implication that small, incremental shifts may occur depending on the situation. The goal of coaching (and therapy, for that matter) is often to increase an individual's internal locus of control, enabling them to own their actions and outcomes of behaviour and to feel less at the whim of others.

attitudes

Attitudes are slightly different. These tend to be more specific than global beliefs; they tend to be concerned with a like or dislike of something in particular and usually emerge from our experiences – or more specifically, our thoughts and emotions about our experiences. The link with behaviour is complex, as many other variables may come into play[3].

The classic example is smoking; we may hold an attitude that smoking is bad for us, yet still indulge. When there is such a disparity with an attitude and behaviour, we are motivated to attempt to reduce it by changing the attitude ('Smoking isn't really that bad for me'), changing the behaviour (stopping or reducing smoking) or rationalising (reframing) the attitude or behaviour ('They're only low tar; there's no history of lung disease in my family; the link with cancer is still unproven'). This uncomfortable tension we feel when our attitudes (or indeed beliefs) and our behaviour are not congruent is called *cognitive dissonance*, a term made famous by Leon Festinger. It is at the heart of our sense of self; a way of rationalising the discrepancies between our actual self and ideal self posited by Carl Rogers in Chapter 8)[4].

There are individual differences in the typical strength of the attitudes we hold, which may be down to personality variables, and in physiological responses (such as a rise in blood pressure) to those attitudes. Think about your own attitude towards, say, fox hunting. How do you feel about it? What are your thoughts about it? How do your thoughts and feelings affect your behaviour in relation to it? It's a useful self awareness exercise to analyse your attitudes like this; separating the affective, cognitive and behavioural components. We have

3 Pratkanis and Turner (1994) argue that the link is stronger when the object of the attitude is well-defined, the strength of the attitude is strong, there is knowledge behind the attitude and when it says something about your identity.

4 It is also the origin of the phrase 'sour grapes' from *The Fox and the Grapes* fable by Aesop. In the story, when a fox can't reach a bunch of grapes he reduces the dissonance by surmising that the grapes are probably sour. Not bad reasoning for a fox.

attitudes because they help us make sense of the world – a cognitive shortcut. They are also an important part of our self identity and personal values, and can determine which social groups we choose to belong to.

changing attitudes

While they are slow to change, attitudes can also be modified by the art of persuasion; if the source of an argument is perceived as credible, trustworthy and expert, and the message itself is credible and well-argued, then attitude change is more likely. The effect is enhanced if both head and heart – cognition and emotion – are addressed.

There's also a link with beliefs here. If we hold the belief that 'we can choose our attitude' – an idea promoted in the book *Fish!*[5] and can instill this in our staff, then we're making real change happen. The premise is that we may not have much of a choice about certain aspects of our role (apart from resigning, of course) but we do have a say in the way we approach the task; again, a reframing exercise.

On a larger scale, a whole organisation's attitudes are often measured through staff surveys, typically looking at staff engagement, job satisfaction and organisational commitment.

knowledge

In some ways, this is the simplest and most obvious area of individual difference. So far we've discussed individual differences in terms of our intellect, our style (personality) and our beliefs and attitudes. Knowledge is the total of the things we know and bring to the job, and the relevant experience we have – although it's important not to confuse the two[6].

In the classic definition of a job competency by Richard Boyatsis – the knowledge, skills and abilities to do your job well – knowledge is separated out from the skills and abilities that are also a function of personality styles and intellect. Knowledge is about things we know; abilities are about applying that

---

5 Lunden, Paul and Christensen (2002).

6 One organisation I worked in wanted to scrap their Long Service awards, as they merely rewarded people sitting in the same organisation (or even job) for years and years, without showing the slightest ambition, development or gumption to move on. It was deemed too controversial to get rid of the awards, which was a shame as doing so would have sent a powerful message that performance was what was valued and rewarded, not just gluing your backside to the chair.

knowledge to actually do something[7]. So knowledge is about the facts and experience that we bring to the table and apply using our intellect and our personality preferences.

In the workplace, acquiring knowledge is all too often equated with going on a training course, and while training is an important source of knowledge it may not always be the most efficient or relevant one. When budgets are tight, other learning options need to be considered, such as: reading, identifying role models, preparing presentations, internal secondments and attachments, stretch assignments and project work, action learning sets, chairing meetings, voluntary work ... the list is endless (see Chapter 6 for more detail).

7 Psychologists often refer to declarative knowledge and procedural knowledge.

chapter 10

motivation

The study of motivation has been fair game for psychologists for years[1], although they by no means have a monopoly on it. It would be wonderful if all this research had told us once and for all what motivates people at work, but like most research it tends to come up with 'Well, it varies. Basically'.

The main problem (or beauty, depending on your point of view) is that we are all individuals, with different intellects, personalities, cultures, past histories and financial circumstances; what motivates one person is not the same as what motivates another. What becomes apparent as you delve into the world of motivation theory is that, as a manager, it's something that you have to actively do something with – it doesn't automatically happen just because you pay someone a salary[2].

To appreciate where we are now with understanding motivation, it's helpful to take a trip back in time and look at where it came from – a journey as much influenced by the psychological paradigms of the time as by the findings of

1 Helped along, no doubt, by funding from the corporate world.

2 But it usually doesn't happen if you don't, to badly misquote Herzberg (see page 80).

the research. An exhaustive look at all the theories would be a book in its own right, so I'll just mention the most influential ones.

scientific management school

After Freud argued that what drives us is essentially unknown to us – because we've either repressed or forgotten the experiences that shaped us[3] – you'll remember that the behaviourists tried to simplify the equation. Internal processes didn't matter, or at least couldn't be studied; what was important (and measurable) was behaviour, a concept seized upon by Frederick Taylor in the first half of the twentieth century.

Here are the roots of time and motion studies and business process re-engineering, born out of the new production line technology at places like Ford. Before the industrial revolution, motivation was primarily all stick and no carrot – you performed in your job because you feared the consequences of not performing. This was rooted in a social relationship; with the rise of large scale industry, ways of increasing mass efficiency became more important and led to the rise of management philosophies.

Taylor pretty much began this movement, in what's known as the scientific management school. In his view inefficiency was a management problem, not a worker problem. Management's job was to select the right people, train them to be efficient, and motivate them by wage incentive schemes.

The prevailing view of the workers at the time was that they were lazy, dim, dishonest and only out for what they could get. Tasks were therefore broken down into repetitive, small, easily trainable chunks, and the workers were set quotas and paid a bonus if they met or exceeded them. The price they paid for undertaking dull work was that they knew the rules and the pay was (relatively) decent – and they had a small window of control over their earnings. The manager's job was to break the job up, set the targets and control the flow because the workers wouldn't have the intellect or interest to do it themselves[4].

theory X and theory Y

I mentioned in Chapter 2 that one psychological paradigm tends to 'create' the next one, in that subsequent paradigms are seen as the antidote. Motivational

3 Unless we pay for psychoanalysis five times a week.

4 Depressing, isn't it?

theories also tend to fall into this pattern. While Taylor was heavily influenced by the behaviourists, by the 1940s and 50s theorists and researchers were busy trying to look into the 'black box', the contents of which the behaviourists said were either unknown or untestable. Understanding these internal processes was now on the agenda, and one well-known theory was very influential in encouraging managers to think outside the (black) box.

Douglas McGregor's concept of dividing managers (and an organisation's prevailing culture) into those that subscribed to *theory X* and *theory Y* is one of the first models that looked at the worker as a 'human resource' instead of something to be exploited:

- **Theory X** (similar to the scientific management belief): workers are lazy, will try to avoid work if they can and need to be closely supervised and coerced).
- **Theory Y**: workers enjoy working, will seek responsibility and meaningful tasks and be to a large part self-managing.

It's true that theory X and theory Y illustrate the two extremes, with most of us being somewhere in between, but McGregor's thinking influenced a raft of motivation theories.

McGregor is describing the two extremes, but does he say which one is best?[5] By best, we mean more motivating and therefore likely to lead to improved performance; ultimately, the point of work-based motivation theories. His argument is that theory Y managers are more likely to generate an atmosphere of trust, growth and development – basic requirements for innovation and the fulfilling of potential. As such, it's hard not to argue that McGregor's call for more of a theory Y culture has shaped human resource strategies today.

hierarchy of needs

Running concurrently with these ideas (and McGregor was in fact influenced by him) were the early formulations of Abraham Maslow's hierarchy of needs theory. It's testament to Maslow's work that most people have at least heard of this, and while it's fair to say that motivation theory has moved on, his ideas still have mileage.

Maslow's focus is what the person brings to the table in terms of motivation, primarily in terms of their needs – what we want from our environment in order to have a motivating effect on our behaviour.

5 Yes.

When we want something, or more accurately have a need for something (two very easily confused concepts!) it creates a sense of disquiet or dissonance. This unpleasant feeling motivates us to restore balance (homeostasis) by fulfilling the particular need. So when our bodies have a need for fuel, we are motivated – by the unpleasant sensation of hunger – to eat and therefore restore balance. Once we're full, we are no longer motivated to perform that particular behaviour – in other words, a satisfied need is not a motivator.

This concept is at the heart of this theory. In addition, Maslow was a humanist, and as such believed in the ultimate worth and capacity for growth of individuals. This positive view of humanity, borne out of his experience as a clinical psychologist, is what influenced McGregor's formulation of theory Y. It also explains the order and nature of Maslow's hierarchy of needs; ultimately, we're motivated by our need for developing our true potential, and this final need – self actualisation – is very much a direction, not an end point.

Maslow's theory states that we all have a set of needs that can be ordered into a hierarchy, or series of levels. As a lower-order need is satisfied, it ceases to become a motivator and our behaviour is then shaped by our desire to satisfy the needs at the next level. The first four levels were termed deficiency needs and must be satisfied before we can focus on our higher-order (self actualisation) needs. This concept has been heavily criticised as being rather ethnocentric and individualistic (societies with a strong collective bias, or those in poverty, would therefore be less likely to be focused on self actualisation needs, and the evidence is simply not there to support these assertions).

The five levels (often depicted as a pyramid with the first one at the bottom) are:

- **Physiological**: these ones are pretty obvious and basic – food, air, water, sleep, sex[6]. In terms of work based factors, this would equate to pay (to provide the food and water), pleasant working conditions and having access to refreshments. Let's forget the sex bit.
- **Safety**: when our physical needs are satisfied, our attention – or more accurately our desire to achieve homeostasis – turns to needs concerned with safety and security. This may be about order, consistency, no alarms and no surprises. At work this may equate to safe (rather than merely pleasant) working conditions, benefits such as pensions or healthcare, job security and insurance policies.

---

6 Although it can be argued that sex permeates all these levels, especially social and esteem needs.

- **Social**: this is about our desire to belong and other emotional aspects such as friends and family, intimacy and acceptance into social groups. This could relate at work to working relationships with individual colleagues and management, and being part of a team. Latest neurological research suggests that this is perhaps even more of a fundamental need than we first realised.
- **Esteem**: this represents our desire to be accepted by others, valued and respected by them and the recognition of our contributions. It also reflects our need for self respect, not just the respect of others. At work this need level may create the desire for a high status job or job title, gaining feedback and recognition for quality work, and getting our opinions respected and listened to.
- **Self actualisation**: the one with no end point. This relates to our desire for growth and advancement, our need to express our creativity and our full potential – everything we are capable of being. To address this need we must have addressed – and in some way fulfilled – the other four levels. Maslow also argues that our genetic potential has a bearing on how this need may manifest. This need relates more to the whole person rather than the work based one, but at work this may include challenge, achievement and development in the role, promotion through the ranks to become the best we can be in whatever we do. Characteristics of such self actualising individuals include increased creativity, spontaneity, autonomy and detachment, a superior sense of reality and an increased identification with the human race[7].

At first glance this may all sound rather simple and reductionist. Maslow, however, did not claim that all of our lower-order needs have to be satisfied before we focus on our higher-order ones. Although no data was collected to support his assertions, Maslow estimated that – at any one time – the average employee has the following percentage of their needs satisfied:

- 85% of their physiological needs
- 70% of their safety needs
- 50% of their social needs
- 40% of their esteem needs
- 10% of their self actualisation needs.

---

7 Leclerc et al (1998) identify 15 characteristics of a self actualising person including: having positive self esteem, are aware of their feelings, are capable of intimate contact and commitment, feel free to express their emotions and take responsibility for their actions. You wouldn't want to meet one.

What's more apparent, however, is that if we're faced with a life-changing situation – such as redundancy or financial loss – then our focus of attention slips down the hierarchy until we again satisfy our immediate physiological and safety needs[8].

One of the most important themes to emerge with Maslow's work is the start of the notion that pay is maybe not the motivator it was originally deemed to be. Yes, it helps satisfy our more basic needs in the hierarchy – paying for food, water and shelter/security needs – but has little impact on the higher-order needs. This idea only increases in prominence as we continue through the timeline of motivation theories.

Building on Maslow's work, Clayton Alderfer in the late 1960s condensed the five levels to three (existence, relatedness and growth – the ERG model) and suggested that we can be actively driven to satisfy our needs at all these evels simultaneously; an assertion that perhaps makes more intuitive and empirical sense.

learned needs

The final need theory we'll discuss is the learned needs theory, developed in the 1950s and 60s by David McClelland. As the name suggests, this theory is slightly different; instead of our needs being intrinsic to us as part of the human condition, our needs are learned from experiences we've had in the culture that we live in, and these experiences affect our perceptions of later events. When we acquire a particular need, we are predisposed to behave accordingly – and differently from those who don't have it.

McClelland identified three major needs as being particularly important. He studied these needs by developing a projective test called the Thematic Apperception Test (TAT). A projective test is one where the individual projects their attitudes, thoughts, desires, etc on to something ambiguous that can have many meanings – the classic example is the Rorschach Inkblot test.

In the TAT, individuals were shown a series of pictures and asked to write a story about them. Some people tended to continually return to the theme of *achievement* (by writing a story about someone striving to meet a goal, for example); others about *affiliation* (their stories concern needing to be with others) and others about influencing and dominating others – the need for

---

8 When you're backpacking in far-off lands, the same thing happens. Where can I find food and shelter? And where's the toilet?

power. These three needs became abbreviated as nAch, nAff and nPow:

- Those with a need for achievement (**nAch**) tend to take personal responsibility for problems, preferring to solve them alone. They set difficult goals and have a strong desire to get feedback from others as to their success or failure on tasks. McClelland found that a high nAch was correlated with managerial success, and while usually emanating from childhood upbringing, could also be learned as an adult. Consequently he developed training in entrepreneurship, and suggested this was how the west could best help poorer countries.
- Those with a high need for affiliation (**nAff**)[9] tend to display a desire for approval and friendship from others, and will look for opportunities at work to satisfy this need. They care about how people feel, value harmony and prefer group, rather than individual, work tasks, enjoying the feeling of being part of a team. They will therefore be motivated by supportive environments with opportunities for social interaction, and if these are provided it is likely to have a positive effect on work performance.
- Those with a strong need for power (**nPow**) have a drive to control the environment around them – which includes other people. They enjoy exercising control over others, will seek positions of leadership and influence and offer their own opinions more than most. With some, the concern is for personal power – dominance for the sake of dominance; for others, the concern is for social power, in which this need presents itself into more group or organisationally focused achievements that have wider benefits than merely ego. McClelland argued that this need for social power is perhaps the most important predictor of being successful as a leader.

So our story started off with the worldview that workers need to be coerced and that the answer to the motivation question is to control them by keeping the job simple and measurable, and reinforce good (profitable) behaviour with pay incentives (Taylor). We then moved on to an alternative model where managers subscribe to one of two opposing worldviews about human nature (McGregor). Theories then started to delve more deeply into what factors, either learned or innate, drive our motivation by way of need fulfilment; we reduce the nasty feeling of an unsatisfied need by being driven to satisfy it (Maslow, Alderfer, McClelland). These need theories help us to understand how individuals differ when faced with similar circumstances.

---

9 Don't titter. I don't think it meant the same then.

job redesign

An alternative to looking at the person, of course, is looking at the job itself. By the 1960s, a researcher called Frederick Herzberg was making a name for himself in the world of job redesign – or more specifically, in how redesigning jobs can improve motivation itself. In a way we've come full circle from Taylor, whose position was that work should be as simple as possible to enable managers to control it (and not spend too much on the training budget), using pay as the principal reward mechanism. Herzberg found that this was far too simple a premise, and distinguished between those factors that were intrinsic to the job itself (*motivating* factors) and those which were extrinsic to the job (*hygiene* factors).

Herzberg discovered through extensive research that satisfaction and dissatisfaction at work were caused by different things (as opposed to simply the opposite or absence of that thing). We are driven to satisfy our hygiene needs – salary, work environment, security, relationships with our fellow workers – because we'd be unhappy without them. However, preventing dissatisfaction in these areas does not lead to a state of satisfaction. In other words, once we've got them we're in a neutral state, not a motivated one.

To be motivated above a baseline level we need satisfaction in factors that are more intrinsic to the job itself – such as achievement, recognition, responsibility and the work itself. Intrinsic motivation is emotional. The emotions of excitement, enjoyment and interest are personal to us and arguably within our control. Think back to when you were last operating at your very best (what some psychologists call 'in a state of flow') and the chances are these emotions were playing a leading role.

The implication of this for designing jobs is profound. If you merely want to prevent your staff being dissatisfied, focus on pay and reward. If you want motivated employees, and the resulting increase in performance, then you need to enrich the job itself. This means providing more scope for autonomy, accountability and responsibility, as far as possible. It means creating truly empowered decision making processes. And it means enabling your staff – through training, coaching and other support mechanisms – to deliver.

To Taylor, then, money is a motivator; probably the most important one. To Herzberg, money is a demotivator if it isn't satisfied, but once a baseline level is reached it won't motivate performance. A pay rise or bonus may have a very short-term effect on performance[10]; but for longer term performance enhancement, enrich (not just enlarge) the job[11].

levels of motivation

A final strand of psychological theory and research into motivation is less to do with individual differences (need theories) or aspects of the job itself, but one based around the factors that influence the level of motivation we demonstrate. In essence this is largely concerned with the interaction between the internal 'push' factors within the individual, and the external 'pull' factors of the job or wider environment. This interaction is a cognitive, thought process; we make rational decisions about how we're going to balance the equation in terms of the exchanges we're prepared to make.

equity theory

The first of these theories is all about balance. In the 1960s, John Adams' equity theory stated that employees are motivated to maintain equity, or a sense of fairness, between what they bring to the table at work (their inputs) and what they get out of it (the outcomes).

Inputs are the time and effort we provide, our experience and qualifications, our loyalty, enthusiasm and commitment and any other contributions we can make to the exchange. Outcomes may include job security, salary and benefits, recognition, responsibility and sense of achievement, as well as praise/thanks[12]. There are obvious links here with the concept of the psychological contract mentioned in Chapter 14. These inputs and outcomes will vary from individual to individual and we all weight these items differently.

This is described as a cognitive theory because we are presumed to make rational choices based on our perceptions of fairness; both in terms of our own sense of justice in terms of our inputs and outcomes, but also in our perceptions of fairness compared to others. We're motivated to seek fair treatment; if we feel we're being treated less favourably when compared to others around us, we're motivated to restore equity, perhaps by reducing our inputs or demanding more outcomes. It can also work the other way; if we

10 Unless you're in a money-oriented job, like sales or banking. Or are a Premier League footballer.

11 Rynes et al (2004) suggest that this link is underestimated, and that people are more motivated by pay than they want others to think.

12 So a footballer may receive the outcome of £150,000 a week for the input of falling over a lot.

perceive that we're getting too much out of the deal compared to others, then our sense of guilt and shame will motivate us to seek balance by increasing our inputs[13].

Because we're dealing with perceptions here, individuals' concepts of what is fair vary, as do the weighting of the various inputs and outcomes. Some may value flexibility of hours higher than level of pay, for example. These perceptions may not always be grounded in reality and a manager may have to help restore the sense of equity by helping people to change their perceptions (of the value of their inputs or those of others – or even the choice of the comparison) as well as actively address the levels of input/outcomes involved. Moreover, we now know that increasing our sense of fairness has an impact on levels of our 'feelgood' chemicals – dopamine, serotonin and oxytocin.

expectancy theories

Finally, there's a raft of theories loosely labelled expectancy theories, and it's worthwhile mentioning these as they have informed a great deal of motivational research. Most seem to originate in work by Victor Vroom in the 1960s. Again, expectancy theory is cognitively based and has similarities with the premise behind equity theory; namely that our behavioural choices are underpinned by mental processes – such as perception and the formation of attitudes – and are primarily motivated by our attempts to maximise pleasure and minimise pain.

In essence, we make these behavioural choices based on our belief that what we do will result in what we intended, and how much we wanted it in the first place. The relationship between these three beliefs – the emotional importance we place on the outcome (*Valence*), our perception of whether our efforts will lead to the desired outcome (*Instrumentality*) and the strength of our belief about whether the outcome is indeed possible (*Expectancy*) – is what is often referred to as VIE theory.

This belief-driven relationship has an impact on our behaviour. If we don't think that our efforts will result in desired behaviour, we'll adjust our efforts accordingly. If we didn't want the outcome in the first place, it had no valence (or does not fit in our value system) and is unlikely therefore to impact positively on behaviour. If we don't think we can successfully perform the task required, our motivation to act is again impeded.

13 More common than redressing it by asking for less pay ...

So according to Vroom, the VIE theory (and its many subsequent iterations) explains why we make the behavioural choices we do. We choose the option with the most motivational force (MF), as this is most likely to cause us pleasure and least likely to cause us pain[14]. The implications for managers are simple:

- First, you need to tap into the emotional component of valence (understand your employee's value systems and work based desires) to ensure that any rewards are actually wanted (ensure Valence).
- Second, you need to ensure your employees have the capacity, capability and confidence to perform at the required level of performance (ensure Expectancy).
- Third, you should ensure that there are clear links between high performance and reward and that those links are understood by the employees (ensure Instrumentality).

In later years, Lyman Porter and Edward Lawler added the variables of actual ability (as opposed to beliefs about ability (expectancy) and role clarity (what they are actually there to do) into the mix; all the motivational effort in the world may not lead to much if there's a lack of ability to perform the job, or a misapprehension as to where it's appropriate to channel the effort.

So that was a potted (and certainly not exhaustive) history of the psychological research into motivation. Some of these theories focus on the internal drivers of the individual, some on the components of the job, and some on the interactions between (and belief systems concerning) the two.

As a Psychological Manager, this is important information to inform your management practice. As we have seen elsewhere[15], tapping into what we are good at and what fires us up has a positive impact on performance, culture/environment and staff turnover rates. In Section five we'll look at what you can practically do to motivate your staff.

---

14 Therefore, $MF = V \times I \times E$.

15 Strengths and the positive psychology movement (see Chapter 2).

section

four

building skill and dealing with will:

facilitating performance and development

about skill and will

Now we understand how individuals differ we can see that the factors determining an individual's *skill* to perform a task is a function of their intelligence, personality preferences and their beliefs, attitudes and knowledge/ experience; what determines their *will* is their motivation (with a dose of attitude thrown in). In this section we learn what you – as a Psychological Manager – can do with this information.

While it could be argued that you are not actually responsible for building skill in your team – only your team members themselves can do that – you are responsible for providing the environment of empowerment and encouragement (and resources) to facilitate that building of skill. It's a subtle difference. And of course you're also responsible for identifying and taking into account the skill levels, both present and potential, in the people who report to you, as well as for dealing with any subsequent performance issues.

As a Psychological Manager you can add the most value from your development attentions by focusing on what most managers appear to be less than proficient at: *quality performance- and development conversations*. In this section we look at the *when*, the *why* and the *how*; when should you be having quality conversations, for what reason, and what enhanced conversational skills you need to develop to become a true Psychological Manager.

the skill/will matrix

When managing the performance and development[1] of your staff, a useful framework on which to base your conversations is the skill/will matrix. Using this framework, you can assess and help build the *skills* of your staff to achieve the goals you are all working towards. You can also assess and build the *will* – or motivation and attitude – of your staff so you can help them perform at their best.

The framework is extremely simple. We can conceptualise whether someone is or isn't performing on a task (or is likely to in the future) by separating their capability on the task and their motivation to do it. There are therefore four possible scenarios:

---

1 The underlying premise of this book is that the two are inseparable. Like Sunday mornings and a cafetiere of rich-roast coffee.

- both a **low current ability** to perform the task and a **low desire** to do so
- a **low current ability** to perform the task but **motivated and willing**
- a **high level of skill** or potential to perform the task but **unwilling**
- a **high level of skill** or potential and **motivated and willing** to do so.

The approach you take when managing the performance and development of the individuals in your team will and should vary depending on where those individuals are in the above framework to perform a task or achieve a goal. The skills they have will depend on past experience, past training and development activities, and an understanding of what the task or role involves and expects[2].

Whether your staff are motivated to perform is rather more complex and will depend on a variety of factors, both personal to the individual and relating to the job or situation itself. Separating these two factors will help you to decide on the most effective approach to the conversations you should be having. This is the essence of the Situational Leadership © model[3]; vary your style of management according to the person and situation you have in front of you.

making a judgement

Imagine this scenario. A meaty piece of work has come in and you want to allocate it to a member of your team. You now understand the skill/will matrix and the theoretical world of individual differences – intellect, personality, beliefs, attitudes and knowledge, and motivation. Where do you go from here?

The obvious first step is to make a judgement. What's your current assessment of your team member's skill (or potential) to perform this task? What support will they need? Will they be motivated? What – as a Psychological Manager – can you do to ensure a successful outcome for everyone involved?

look for evidence

The best predictor of future job performance is (drum roll) past performance. What evidence do you have of that person's past performance on similar tasks? It helps to have a reasonably thorough understanding of what this piece of work entails so you can break it down into its constituent parts. You can then look back for evidence (or transferable skill evidence) that can help you make the judgement call.

2 Note that this has little to do with mere length of time in the job ...

3 *The One Minute Manager* series by Ken Blanchard and others.

Looking for evidence (this may involve getting feedback from others who have insights into the individual's working practices) can help to dismiss any explicit or indeed unknown prejudices you may hold about that person and their own attempts at impression management. It also helps to be as specific as possible about the task itself.

After finding any appropriate evidence and other people's perspectives, the next step is to have an honest conversation with the individual concerned. Ask them about similar work they've done before and what level of support they feel they'll need.

performance management skills

Your assessment of the individual's current skill level is an important factor in determining your initial leadership style for them on this task (more on leadership style in Chapter 14).

top three skills

This leadership style is ideally based on a blend of a set of tools that the Psychological Manager has at their disposal; to badly misquote Brian Clough[4], I wouldn't say they are the best three management skills to have, but they are in a shortlist of three. 'They' are:

- goal setting
- feedback
- coaching.

The first three chapters of this section look at each of these in turn, before dealing with will – or motivation – in Chapter 14.

---

4 Brian Clough, for anyone either under 30 or who has no interest in football, was an English football manager (Derby County, Nottingham Forest) in the 1970s and 80s. He was played by Michael Sheen in the 2009 film *The Damned United* about his disastrous time at Leeds United. He is famous for his rather maverick approach to football management and his managerial quotes. My favourite four (in a shortlist of four) are:

- 'I wouldn't say I was the best manager in the business. But I was in the top one';
- 'We talk about it for twenty minutes and then we decide I was right';
- 'The river Trent is lovely; I know because I have walked on it for eighteen years';
- 'Rome wasn't built in a day. But I wasn't on that particular job'.

Priceless.

the essence of performance management

Goal setting seems to be an accepted way of operating in today's workplace, ever since Peter Drucker's work in the 1950s on Management by Objectives (MBO). An essential part of this was the monitoring of standards against some clearly defined criteria; the very essence of performance management.

Put simply, performance management is about getting results. It's about getting the best out of people and helping them achieve their potential – and through them, the potential of the organisation. It's not merely an annual appraisal, but the embedding of an ongoing dialogue of structured performance-related conversations and interventions that steers behaviour towards meeting organisational goals.

These goals and objectives should then be reviewed at regular one-to-ones (arguably monthly) to discuss progress and to help deal with any obstacles or identify any emerging development needs. Two key skills here are required of the Psychological Manager:

- adopting a coaching approach to performance management (there's a plethora of literature outlining the empowering, motivational and developmental by-products of coaching)
- giving constructive feedback on an ongoing basis (this underpins the whole performance management process).

These two elements often require a cultural shift in managers' understanding of their role, and require adequate training and support. The giving of feedback may range from simple conversations covering 'what's going well and what needs to be done differently', to online 360 degree feedback instruments.

The simple concept behind these ideas is that when it comes to the annual appraisal/performance and development review, there should be no surprises. Both the manager and the member of staff are already aware of performance successes and any difficulties that have occurred over the last 12 months and have taken appropriate steps to address them.

The view that performance management is somehow synonymous with 'managing poor performers out' is anathema to creating a healthy, learning culture. It requires a managerial workforce that is skilled in the basic 'conversational' elements of management such as constructive feedback and coaching practice – and uses these skills continuously – to effectively embed any such cultural shift.

chapter 11

goalsetting

As we'll see later, goal setting is an important part of the coaching process. For now, though, let's keep it separate until we merge it with coaching in Chapter 13.

There's also an obvious link between goal setting and motivation[1], which can't be underestimated. Indeed the seminal writers on the subject, Gary Latham and Edwin Locke, suggest that the relatively straightforward concept and technique of goal setting may be more of a motivator than the usual suspects of money and job enrichment. It's also a tried and tested one – goal setting first rears its head in the scientific management school of Frederick Taylor (see Chapter 10).

1 Arnold and Randall et al (2010) suggest 'Difficult and specific goals have this effect [better performance] by focusing a person's attention on the task, increasing the amount of effort they put into it, increasing the length of time they keep trying, and encouraging the person to develop strategies for goal achievement.'

benefits of setting goals

The benefits of taking time to design organisational, team and individual goals and objectives are often implicitly assumed. Let's make them explicit. Goals provide direction; something to aim for that taps into a larger vision. They break down the larger vision (it doesn't have to be a BHAG[2]) into clear steps that make that vision appear less daunting. They give you some measures of success along the way – milestones – that help keep motivation and commitment up when working towards a longer-term vision. They can also help every member of the team understand their part in the jigsaw, and have an awareness of everyone else's.

At the heart of Latham and Locke's assertions are three key points that are still regarded as universal truths when it comes to goal setting:

- Difficult but achievable goals are more motivating – and lead to higher performance – than those that are too simple or easily achieved. They argue that our natural desire for challenge is the key factor here.
- Goals that are specific as opposed to vague again lead to improved performance as it makes the task clear (and more conducive to receiving feedback).
- Goals that are set *with* the individual, rather than *for* the individual, tend to lead to the setting of higher goals and more commitment to achieve them, as they are internally accepted by the individual[3].

To make any goal happen, we need a plan. Without plans and clear definitions of success, our best intentions fall by the wayside[4]. This is an essential part of the coaching model and we'll go through a format to help it happen. It's also one of Stephen Covey's 7 habits: 'Begin with the end in mind' (habit 2)[5]. This means understanding the destination before you start the journey, leading to great

---

2 James Collins and Jerry Porras in their book *Built to Last* talk about successful organisations having big dreams which are unifying catalysts for team spirit, such as Microsoft's 'a computer on every desk and in every home'. They called these visions BHAGs, or Big Hairy Audacious Goals. Yes, really.

3 Haslam et al (2009) dispute this, suggesting that participation in setting goals and objectives is not always necessary. Most argue the opposite.

4 Such as New Year's resolutions. One of the reasons that the third Monday in January is called Blue Monday is that by then most people have broken their 1 January pledge. And it's dark and cold. And 11 months till Christmas.

5 *The 7 Habits of Highly Effective People* (2004).

coaching questions such as 'What does good look like?' and 'How would you define success on this goal?'

Effective people know where they want to get to, have visualised the end goal and gained commitment by understanding how it relates to wider goals and objectives. You need to help your team do the same with the goals you set with them by helping them understand how the particular task contributes to the bigger picture or vision/mission statement.

Recently goal setting theory has been influenced by social cognitive schools of thought. These theories suggest that goals provide people with cognitive representations or maps of whatever outcomes are needed on a task. We then analyse the gap between the goal's current and desired future state, which affects our perceptions, thoughts and coping strategies such as motivational (or otherwise) self talk.

Goals in which we are learning, rather than merely performing, also appear to produce higher performance. Farr et al distinguished between learning goal orientation and performance goal orientation: in the former, we're concerned with improving our competence; in the latter, with demonstrating our competence. As mentioned at the beginning of this section, performance and development are inextricably linked.

The message here for the Psychological Manager is that the closer you can align your team's performance goals with their personal development, the more commitment and resulting performance improvement you are likely to see. Aiming for a goal has a motivational effect; the positive expectations it creates increases levels of dopamine, a primary mood-enhancing chemical.

SMART goal setting model

The standard 'how to' model of goal/objective setting (from now on I'll use these terms interchangeably) is the SMART model. This stands for:

- **Specific**: Exactly what is it that is to be achieved? Specific goals are clear, unambiguous, written in the positive[6], and focus on output rather than actions. You should avoid phrases like *improve relationships, keep up to date, communicate better* and other such vague generalisations. You may want to ask yourself questions like *who, what, where, how* specifically, and most importantly, *what* the goalee's part is in the achievement of the goal[7].

---

6 i.e. not 'avoid failure'.

7 'Goalee' is a made-up word. It's not going to win any awards.

By including the *when* – covered under T for Time-bound – we have what in neuro linguistic programming terms is called a *well-formed outcome*. In any event, it's better for them (clarity) and for you (easier for performance management purposes).

- **Measurable**: How will you know whether you are achieving the goal? How will anyone else know – what will they see? This does not have to be particularly onerous but being able to measure success against some form of yardstick helps with motivation and helps ensure you're on track, removing any misinterpretation or subjectivity. This could also include milestones along the way, again breaking a bigger, scarier goal into more easily achievable chunks. This is often difficult, but attempt to get some form of numerical measure for the goal – it concentrates the mind! Remember – what gets measured gets done ...
- **Achievable**: The goal should be technically possible, be stretching (see Latham and Locke above) and require effort and a sense of challenge. A goal that's too hard (*I want you to give 110%*) is demotivating and will tend to be ignored, while one that's too easy (*I want you to make at least two sales calls this month. If you have time. And can be bothered*) does not lead to higher performance. Goals that are not accepted as achievable by the goalee may reflect their own confidence levels, so check what support is necessary.
- **Relevant**: Some authors call this one Realistic, but that's pretty well covered under Achievable. The point here is that the goal should have a point. Does this goal help your department or team achieve what it's there to do? Does it fit in with the overall mission? What impact will it have? Having a goal that fits in with departmental objectives is not only important for the department, it makes the goalee feel that they are contributing to the bigger picture – that their role/effort/behaviours are worthwhile. It's good practice to continually ask yourself and your team 'Why are we doing this, exactly?'
- **Time-bound**: Effective goals have milestones set along the way and have a definite end point or deadline. A set date for completion concentrates the mind; milestones along the way doubly so[8]. Some people find an end date motivating, others find it constraining and stressful (see Chapter 19 for the different personality characteristics measured by the MBTI ©). However, a goal without a deadline is like a broken pencil[9]. Or, at least, other things get done first. And as goals are rarely separate from the rest of the department's

8 New Year's resolutions don't work not only because they're usually too vague, but also because a year is just too long.

9 Pointless. Apologies to Blackadder.

(or organisation's) goals, there can be unintended knock-on effects if those deadlines are not set, or if they are missed or badly chosen in the first place.

So goals should be difficult but achievable, they should be specific not vague (write them down), and they should be ideally set with, not for, the individual concerned. They should include numbers and behaviours. They should be SMART, they should be simple, and there shouldn't be too many of them; working on too many goals or objectives at the same time dilutes effort.

As a manager, you can work with your team to ensure relevance and set priorities, and agree a system of monitoring that's right for the particular individual and situation – the essence of Situational Leadership © (see Chapter 14). Finally, make sure you and your team constantly review these goals for relevance, for achievability and for timeliness.

chapter 12

feedback

I hope it's obvious by now that an essential part of the review process should include the provision of constructive feedback. In engineering terms, feedback is a process whereby a portion of an output is routed back to the input to either increase it or change it in some way. Its name has been given to a written or conversational process whereby an individual gains awareness of how their outputs (behaviours) have had an impact on the external world of people and things, with a view to reinforcing or changing those behaviours.

Feedback is one of the most powerful tools in the Psychological Manager's toolkit. Its purpose is to improve performance, enhance learning and help generate motivation. Note that the point is about change in the receiver of feedback. It should not be about reducing tension in the giver who wants to 'get things off my chest' – any benefit should be primarily for the one on the receiving end. At its best it empowers people to change, because we can't control what we're not aware of.

There are many reasons why you as a Psychological Manager may desire to give feedback. You may notice things yourself about how your staff are performing or behaving, or you may have received feedback from elsewhere. You may wish to review a project or discrete piece of work, or give feedback on a presentation, meeting or client interaction. The point is we don't give nearly enough of it. A feedback culture, where the giving and receiving of constructive feedback is routine and expected, is a healthy culture.

constructive feedback

Note the emphasis on the magic word in feedback terms: *constructive*. Feedback should be about changing or reinforcing behaviour; it facilitates that change by motivating the individual to change, and is therefore future focused. It's the difference between *this is what you could do differently* and *you should have done this, this and this*. It has a different impact on the receiver – one that's more likely to result in behaviour change.

As with all conversational aspects of managing, any feedback session is influenced by the nature of the relationship you have and the rapport that has been built between you. As such, it's important not to just drop feedback on an unsuspecting party if that's not the culture you've engendered with your team. There may be a little bit of background work (or at least a warning that you're going to start encouraging feedback) to do before launching your finely tuned feedback skills on your unsuspecting team.

Having an idea of ground rules may help (face-to-face whenever possible, perhaps followed up in writing if appropriate) so your team will know what to expect. Best practice suggests that you create a culture whereby your team feels they can also give you feedback; in that way you are role-modelling the behaviours you wish to see.

Constructive feedback, then, facilitates behavioural change. It helps engender an atmosphere of trust, and an atmosphere of trust helps reduce our natural inclination to defensiveness when receiving feedback. Most of us have received badly given feedback at one point in our lives, and can remember how it made us feel. As such, we may have the residual schema left over – that voice in our head which says 'prepare for attack'. We then meet that feedback with 'Yes, but ...' responses and other attempts to justify our performance or behaviour, which reduces our capacity to reflect on how we might do things differently. Receiving feedback is potentially a threat to our perception of status!

So what does constructive feedback look like?

focused

First and foremost, constructive feedback focuses on *behaviour*, not the person. And not just generalised behaviour either, but specifics, such as:

- What precisely was good about the behaviour?
- What precisely is it that you want to see done differently?
- How might it be improved?
- What would that improvement look like and what development steps are needed?

An example may help here. Instead of saying 'You aren't very good at presenting' – because this focuses on the person, is likely to be taken personally and defensively, and is vague in its scope – you could structure the feedback in the following terms:

- What went well ('Your body posture was open and positive in that you faced the audience at all times')
- What didn't go so well ('You read verbatim from notes, which had the resulting impact of losing rapport with the audience and made it look like you didn't know your subject or lacked confidence')
- What could have been done differently ('You could have read bullet points from your cue cards instead of writing the whole presentation out and then merely reading it. This would have the impact of making you appear more confident and more engaging with the audience').

All this helps to avoid what is known in the world of feedback as the Barnum effect[1]. This approach to feedback is future focused in that it helps improve performance in the future, is specific as opposed to woolly, and looks for solutions instead of blame or mere criticism.

---

1 The Barnum effect is not a morbid fear of being played by Michael Crawford. It's the same person, though. P.T. Barnum was an American showman and owner of a circus in the 1800s. One of the sayings attributed to him derived from his advertising slogan for his circus, 'We've got something in it for everyone'. So in feedback terms a Barnum statement is one that's so vague that it gains false agreement – the statement has something in it for everyone. Less than robust personality questionnaires fall into this trap ('Under huge amounts of pressure, you may find yourself getting slightly anxious') as do horoscopes ('If today is your birthday, there may be some cake appearing in your life'). I'm naturally biased against horoscopes, though. Part and parcel of being a Pisces.

clear impact

As was touched on in the example above, the impact the behaviour had should be made clear. The way someone performs or the actions and behaviours they exhibit are not the same as the effect they may have on the recipient. By clarifying impact as well as behaviour, you're making the link explicit – thereby answering the 'What for?' question[2].

We can get so wrapped up in the complexities of a task that we can forget or not even notice the effect we may be having on others. I always make a point of asking first, rather than telling – for example, 'What impact did you think that behaviour had?' If the observation first comes from the recipient[3] this is a far more powerful motivator for change.

balanced

Constructive feedback is also balanced. Many people have a biased view of feedback, assuming that it's about being told what they did wrong – usually fed from experiences they've had of poor practice in the past. We aren't talking about the 'Say something good, hide the bad bit in the middle, then say something good to cheer them up a bit' approach[4] – people see through this fairly quickly. But we do need to ensure that our feedback has both what went well (behaviours to keep and be reinforced) and what didn't go so well (behaviours to change/avoid/develop). The strengths based approach goes a step further and absolutely focuses more on what went well and how those behaviours could be 'translated' across to other scenarios, or combined with other strengths.

timely

Finally, constructive feedback is timely. It's not good practice to save up a list of things to give feedback on, and then dump them on the poor individual at appraisal time. Good feedback is given as soon after the event as is practically possible, at a time when you can have a private, uninterrupted one-to-one conversation. The longer you leave it, the less it will be thought of as being in the present moment and therefore not a priority for change.

---

2 i.e. this is *why* your behaviours need to change; it has *this* impact on others.

3 The coaching approach to feedback suggests that you always ask the recipient first, before giving your own views.

4 Known in feedback terms as 'the sh*t sandwich'.

giving constructive feedback

The 'how to do it' is the simple bit. At its most elegant, constructive feedback is covered in three statements:

- This is what you did well on this piece of work
- This is what you could have done differently to make it even better
- This is how I can support your development in this area.

However, I prefer to take more of a coaching approach to giving feedback, which is essentially saying the same things as above, but starting each part with the recipient's view first. So our feedback session becomes:

- What do you think/feel went well generally?
- What do you think/feel *you* did well? (then add your own/others' observations and explore similarities/differences in viewpoint as well as the impact the behaviours had).
- What could you have done differently/how would you do it differently if you were going to do it again? (again, then adding your own and others' views and the impact).
- What support do you need to address these development needs/play to your strengths even more?
- What's the first step to achieving this?

360 degree feedback

Any conversation about feedback isn't complete without mentioning 360 degree feedback. Sometimes called multi-source feedback, this is simply a process (usually online these days) for creating conversations about how individuals are perceived by their colleagues. It improves self awareness of strengths and weaknesses by identifying how those strengths and weaknesses impact on others. The feedback process mentioned earlier is a conversation between two people – you as manager, them as direct report. By using 360 degree feedback this conversation opens out to a variety of sources of information.

The principle is simple. It typically involves the receiver of the feedback identifying a set of people whose opinions are valued and who are aware how they work and interact. These people are usually put into categories (boss, peers, any direct reports and themselves – and sometimes even clients/customers[5]) and any responses grouped accordingly. It's therefore possible to determine whether all these groups have the same views on the receiver's strengths and weaknesses as the receiver does.

These respondents may be asked to rate the receiver on competencies, or simply provide their views on what the individual does well and could do differently (usually a combination of the two are used). Individual responses are anonymised, so that the receiver of the feedback is aware of what themes have emerged, but not the specific source. This helps ensure that people are more honest; however, in the healthiest feedback cultures respondents are happy to give their names to the specific comments they make.

When all the data is collected, a confidential feedback session takes place (for best practice, using a fully trained facilitator in a face-to-face meeting) and the respondent is encouraged to share the themes with their manager. This subsequent conversation can help the receiver of feedback make sense of it in an organisational context and clarify next steps towards making the most of the identified strengths, and developing the weaknesses if deemed appropriate.

There's a large and growing amount of evidence for the benefits of promoting 360 degree feedback as an important element of a feedback culture[6]. It can dramatically improve self awareness, especially when we realise that our own views of our working style or competence are not shared by others. We rarely get this sort of information by any other means. It can also help promote cultural change by providing a tangible process for openness and transparency. As long as you don't do it in isolation from other initiatives (such as links with development opportunities and action planning[7]), provide skilled

---

5 Interestingly, and somewhat obviously, direct report ratings tend to be the most accurate, but we pay more attention to what the boss says.

6 However, there are mixed views about linking it to formal appraisal processes. It can tend to produce blandness of responses as no-one wants to be so honest that it affects people's pay rises ...

7 It's very demoralising to go through this process, which can be quite scary, and not be offered any development support afterwards. This is tantamount to saying 'We think you're rubbish at this aspect of your work and we're not going to help you change it'.

facilitation, and use a well-constructed, relevant instrument, 360 degree feedback can be a powerful performance management and development tool[8].

The main point behind all this is that it should be perfectly possibly to give feedback on something that isn't going well and still maintain a positive relationship and the self esteem of the recipient. By doing so, you're helping to illuminate any blind spots the individual has and facilitating their development – and hence performance. And by role-modelling excellent feedback practice, you're also facilitating real culture change.

8 Usually the management development programmes I design kick off with a 360 degree feedback assessment, and – when budgets allow – finish with one, too. There's no better way to add focus and clarity to a long-term development initiative (IMHO).

chapter 13

coaching

When we talk about cultural change, however, this is the big one. Coaching goes hand-in-hand with goal setting and feedback; so much so that the three are inexorably linked. If you can create a culture where SMART goal setting, the giving and receiving of feedback, and routine coaching conversations are the norm, then you're truly on your way to being a Psychological Manager.

Of course I'm not talking about setting yourself up as a coach and going through a formal accredited course (although this is a great idea if it interests you!). Here I'm talking about using coaching skills and frameworks to facilitate better managerial conversations. The skills, frameworks and processes are the same – it's just a matter of degree.

When you operate within a coaching culture at work, it merely means that instead of having your default as solving people's problems for them or directing their work by telling them what to do, you're helping them to solve their own problems through structured, empowering conversations – thereby improving both performance and development. And while initially it may take more, rather than less of your time, ultimately it pays dividends.

Taking a coaching approach to your line management is not a quick-fix one, and it inevitably means spending more time with your direct reports than if you simply directed them. But that's not the point. Coaching empowers, develops and enriches those who report to you like nothing else can, and it ultimately leads to better performance as people learn to solve their own problems. It's also empowering, developmental and enriching for you[1]. Both parties are learning, and through them the organisation does, too.

In my experience, the greatest barrier to having successful coaching-style conversations as part of your performance and development process is one of *attitude*. The problem isn't usually an unwillingness to be coached: more often it's the managers' attitudes – either they don't believe coaching has value or is the right way to approach these conversations, or say that they don't have the time. Once you really believe that coaching can add value to your managerial toolkit, the rest is relatively easy.

the concept of coaching

So let's clarify what coaching as a concept is. While there are many styles and models/frameworks to choose from, they are all largely facilitative in style; coaching is an exercise in facilitation, not teaching or directing. These various approaches therefore are all *process* led rather than *content* led, and are based on a supportive, constructive relationship through the medium of conversation.

Most writers suggest coaching originates in the world of sport, although anyone who's had ski *instruction* knows that it tends to be precisely that. It was Timothy Gallwey who applied coaching as an approach to tennis[2] and then in the wider organisational setting that helped popularise it. In fact the business world embraced coaching, while the sports world tended to leave it behind and stick to teaching rather than facilitating.

Coaching, then, is about helping people to learn through unlocking their potential, not mentoring them or teaching them all you know[3]. It requires expertise in the technique, not the subject, and its aims – according to the guru of the model we'll explore later, John Whitmore – is to generate awareness, responsibility and self belief in the coachee.

1 I learnt more as a coach when working at the BBC about the BBC itself and about managing staff than a plethora of courses could have taught me.

2 'The opponent within one's head is more formidable than the one the other side of the net.'

3 Until I really understood what coaching was, I used to wonder why – sticking with tennis – someone like Roger Federer needed a coach.

By building awareness, we give our coachee some control back; we can't control what we're not aware of. Through focused attention, questioning and reflecting we can help our coachee be more tuned in to the essence of their problem – and potential solutions. By building responsibility, we're making it clear that the answer to their problem lies within them and that the choices they make are theirs, no-one else's. When we tell someone what to do, or even give our best-intentioned advice, we unwittingly take on some of that responsibility without the power to do anything with it[4].

Finally, by ensuring that successes are seen to be coming from the coachee not the coach, and that they are trusted and feel empowered within and by the relationship, we facilitate self belief in our coachee. We can help them see the link between their solutions and choices and the impact of those choices – and help them see what was successful so they can apply the learning elsewhere. NLP practitioners talk about being 'at cause' – identifying the part of the problem that is your responsibility or within your power to change, and focusing on that.

mentoring

Coaching and mentoring are often talked about in the same manner, but there are some fundamental differences between them[5]. Mentoring is similar to role modelling. It's a bit like having an older brother or sister[6], giving advice and practical help, sharing networks and providing organisational or professional context and knowledge.

In its pure sense, coaching is more performance and development driven as opposed to the wider remit of 'this is how we do things around here'. Coaching conversations don't really include advice. Indeed, you need know nothing about the topic concerned to have an effective coaching conversation; it's the

4 Anyone who's ever advised a mate to dump their girlfriend/boyfriend will be all too aware of the blame and years of snide comments that can be attached to this strategy.

5 And similarities – I teach coaching skills to mentors. While it's a different concept, many of the interpersonal skills are the same.

6 Without the arm pinching and having to tell your mum.

process, not the knowledge of the topic that's important[7]. If anything, being an expert in the topic can get in the way, because the knowledge can be imposed or overused. The attitude/orientation of trust is relevant here – it's not just about having trust in the coachee that they have the answers; it's also about trusting yourself and trusting the process.

benefits

There are many reasons why you should use coaching in the workplace. We're brought up with command-and-control style management (parents, school, sports) so this tends to be our mental map or our default position because it's been hardwired into us through these experiences.

However, command-and-control doesn't really work that well with adults, as many dictators have found. We don't remember things as effectively when we're told, as opposed to when we've experienced them for ourselves. We don't perform to goals as readily when they are imposed. If we accept that a manager's job is to get the task done and retain/grow their team, then coaching hits both spots. It's not always the best approach (pure knowledge transfer when time is of the essence is not a recipe for a coaching conversation[8]) but it is a great one for your toolkit. And one in which you learn, too. Win/win.

Being coached gives us our calm space. It can help us reduce the emotional arousal we experience about events, or threats to our status or independence, and allows us to start engaging the thinking parts of our brain. Somewhat ironically, the act of problem solving with someone else can also stop us from overthinking a problem, and allow us to express the more subtle insights we may have. And as our coach is a step removed from the issue, their insights may also be tentatively added to the mix.

---

7 This is a big myth of coaching. As a coach, I used to have coaching conversations about making programmes at the BBC without ever having made a programme. If in doubt at this early stage, look at the Socratic questions mentioned on pages 107–108. None of them require any knowledge of the subject, but answering them really helps generate understanding or – as we'll go on to clarify – awareness and responsibility. John Whitmore gives the example of running out of tennis coaches, so he got ski coaches to put on tennis outfits and act as coaches. They were indistinguishable – if anything, some of them were better than the original tennis coaches. The expertise needed is in coaching techniques, not the subject.

8 Such as 'What do we really want to achieve out of this alarm/fire exit scenario?'

coach vs manager

All of this sounds fair enough if you're someone's coach, but this book is for managers who want to improve the quality of their conversations. Can a manager really be a coach to their direct report? The answer is: it depends.

There are many benefits to having the space and freedom a fully independent coach can bring. This is expensive, however, and so tends to be the preserve of managers themselves; there's money to be made in executive coaching. So here we aren't talking about being your direct report's coach per se; we're more concerned with having routine coaching conversations as part of your managerial responsibilities.

Coaching requires an ability to be detached and to be able to recognise and wear different hats at different times; now coach, now mentor/role model, now manager. Being aware of the differences in terms of skills and responsibilities and practising switching between them is key – as is your attitude. If you believe a coaching approach is the most effective intervention to facilitate performance improvement and development in your staff, then you'll find opportunities to do so[9].

create the culture

So much of coaching is about your attitude rather than skills per se. Yes, using a coaching framework (see pages 109–116) and having great rapport building, questioning and summarising/reflecting skills are important, but if you really don't subscribe to the philosophy that people have all the resources they need internally to solve their own problems, then you'll limit the effectiveness and impact of your coaching conversations. You really have to mean it.

So to create a coaching-inspired performance culture is to create one with plenty of trust, commitment to the process, and belief in both yourself as coach and in your coachee. This last one is the hard one[10]. In Chapter 10

9 If you are relatively new to this, it's a good idea to position it first with your team. If they're used to a more directive style, and you suddenly start trying to coach them out of the blue, you can meet with some scepticism or resistance. Pave the way first – 'I thought we'd try a different approach from normal – are you willing to give it a go?'

10 I'm reminded of a scene in Ridley Scott's 2000 film *Gladiator*, when someone asks Russell Crowe what it takes to be as good a gladiator as him. He gives the first two reasons as a sharp sword and plenty of practice (I may be paraphrasing here), and the third as not caring if you live or die. It's always the third one that's the problem.

we discussed Douglas MacGregor's theory X (workers are lazy and need to be closely supervised) and theory Y (workers seek responsibility and are largely self managing). We also mentioned that 'theory Y managers are more likely to generate an atmosphere of trust, growth and development – basic requirements for innovation and the fulfilling of potential'. If you subscribe to a theory X of management and human nature in the wider sense, it's hard to see how you can facilitate the creation or maintenance of a coaching culture.

skilled questioning

It will be clear by now that at the heart of a coaching conversation is the concept of skilled questioning. A useful belief to hold is one where asking a question creates a vacuum and the answer will rush to fill it. While this may not physically be happening, mentally it's as good a metaphor as any.

Whitmore explains the power of questioning over telling by using a tennis example. Anyone learning any ball game will hear the phrase 'watch the ball' from those teaching them. If only it were that simple. Simply being told to do it doesn't seem to translate into action. Instead, Whitmore argues, it's far more effective to ask a question which means you have to watch the ball to answer it. Such a question creates focus, there's no judgement involved, and the results can be tested by the coach.

Examples are: 'Which way is the ball spinning as it comes to you?' and 'How high is the ball as it comes over the net?' To the coach, the answer isn't really that important. To the coachee, it is prompting behavioural change or insight – awareness and responsibility.

Socratic questioning

Socrates claimed that he was a 'midwife to understanding' – in other words, he didn't teach the understanding but he helped bring it into the world. It's no coincidence that Socratic questioning – structured, deep questioning used to break down and explore complex ideas – is at the heart of a coaching approach. Classic approaches to Socratic questioning concern:

- Achieving clarity ('What causes you to believe that?')
- Challenging assumptions ('What makes you think that is true in this case?')
- Clarifying evidence ('What evidence do you have to support that assertion?')
- Seeing alternatives ('How else could you get that effect?')
- Considering implications ('What do you think the effect on xxx would be?')

- Questioning the process itself ('What part of this discussion have you found useful? What will you do differently as a result of it?')

This is as far from merely directing or telling as it's possible to get; unfortunately, it's more difficult giving up the ego-boost of telling than it is to learn how to be a coach.

open questions

Open questions are of far more use than closed ones here (although the latter can be used to help open up an area for discussion or merely get the ball rolling) and can start broadly ('Tell me more about that') and drill down into more detail as appropriate ('So what specifically was the result?').

They may also go the other way (what some coaches call *chunking up* – 'So what is that an example of?') if the coach is trying to help the coachee extract themselves from detail. Leading questions are best avoided[11], as are those beginning with 'why' as they tend to be heard judgementally and responded to defensively.

listening

I mentioned above that the answer to some of these questions is not really that important to the coach – but it's more accurate to say that it's of less importance than it is to the coachee. In formulating an answer, the coachee has had to crystallise a thought which hitherto was floating in the ether; the act of answering has made it more tangible and concrete.

Even paraphrasing what the coachee has said – reflecting back in your own words – can have an immensely powerful effect as it may not have been heard 'out loud' by the coachee before. Paying attention to the answers will of course help you form a clearer picture of the issue and help to channel the conversation, but always remember that you are primarily asking the question to generate awareness in your coachee, not for your own interest.

You most definitely have to demonstrate that you are listening, however. Apart from generating trust and building rapport, listening is an essential component of empathy[12]. Most coaches have fallen into the trap of formulating their next question – like a TV news reporter – while the coachee is answering the last one. The coachee will spot this[13].

11 'What was it that first attracted you to the millionaire Paul Daniels?'

12 Empathy is a combination of getting into the frame of reference of someone else and demonstrating that you are doing so.

13 I used to be a telephone counsellor for people in distress. It never ceased to amaze me how a caller, particularly one in dire straits, would notice this even during a period of silence.

The usual rules of rapport building apply when you are listening: open body language and posture, appropriate eye contact and facial expressions – both checking your own and noticing what is going on in your coachee[14]. Some useful and powerful challenges can be made by making a call on the incongruity between the words people use and their tone of voice and body language.

coaching framework: the GROW model

So far we've looked at what coaching is, why it's good for you and good for your team, why your attitude is key, and identified some important skills such as questioning, listening and attending, and building rapport to demonstrate empathic understanding. The actual 'how we do it' is far more straightforward; one of the most widely used yet effective frameworks is also one of the simplest, providing a clear four-stage route map through a structured coaching conversation. This framework is the GROW model, made famous by John Whitmore in *Coaching for Performance*.

Let's say I want to get fitter. If you ask me questions to help me get fitter, most of them will fall into the same category: 'What's your diet like?', 'How much weight do you want to lose?', 'What sports do you like?', 'What have you tried so far?' and so on. These are all good, useful coaching-style questions.

But what they lack is context. We mentioned this when talking about goal setting and New Year's resolutions in Chapter 11; without knowing what 'fit' looks like to me, the whole concept lacks specificity. It's far better to start with a set of questions getting me to clarify what fit means to me, what I want to do with it[15], and how specifically you can help me[16]. This is the same idea as Stephen Covey's habit 2: 'Begin with the end in mind' (see page 91). Identify what you want and work backwards.

John Whitmore has provided a framework to do just this. His useful sequence of questions adds structure and direction to what can feel like a very unstructured and ambiguous process. You don't have to follow it slavishly, but it certainly helps to keep it in the back of your mind to stop your well-intentioned coaching conversation becoming a nice cosy chat.

The fact that you're using a framework doesn't have to be made explicit to your coachee, and it doesn't have to get in the way of an informal problem solving

---

14 We listen with our eyes, too.

15 i.e. running a marathon in under four hours, or running up the stairs without getting out of breath.

16 i.e. by the end of this session I'd like to have three ideas to take away and research.

exchange. You can even coach yourself on a problem by going through the sequence in a few minutes, which is actually a good way to practise. Somewhat obviously, the four stages go by the acronym GROW.

G is for Goal

In longer-term coaching relationships, this may relate to the overall topic for the intervention as a whole; for example, people have been 'sent' to me for coaching on their delegation skills over four to six sessions. It's important to remember, however, that the topic is not the goal. The goal or goals for the intervention need to be clarified in terms of end goals (the ultimate reason they have come for coaching) and performance goals (effectively a series of SMART objectives (see Chapter 11) that relate to achieving the end goal).

In more immediate 'one-off with follow-up' coaching conversations that you initiate as a manager, the focus may be more about the goal for that particular session. This may be something like 'a way forward and the first steps towards identifying and solving the problem' or 'a list of action points to take away'.

Here's how such a session may start. Your direct report asks for a meeting to discuss some problems they're having with a project. What happens most of the time is that they go into a monologue about the problems they're facing and expect you to come up with solutions. Of course, as we have seen, some problems may require just that if the answer is simply a quick knowledge transfer, is urgently required or if there's absolutely no margin for error.

However, if the issue is more in depth and you've been asked for help, there is another way. Starting the conversation off with a G-related question helps to set the tone for the meeting and really start with the end in mind. It also puts the responsibility for the solution rightly back on the coachee. An example question might be 'We have half an hour together; what would you like to leave this meeting with?' or 'What would you like to get out of this meeting?' – or (my personal favourite) 'What would success look like in thirty minutes?'

Depending on the response you get, you may have to help the coachee focus on specific outcomes that are reasonable in the timeframe allowed. Again, the SMART mnemonic helps. Going back to my 'I want to get fitter' example, the longer-term goal constitutes what fit means and looks like, by when and to do what – and how I'll know when I've achieved it. If my response to your opening question 'What does fit look like?' was to run a marathon in full badger costume in less than four hours, your job is to help me ascertain whether this is a reasonable – i.e. achievable – goal in the timeframe allowed.

The session also needs a short-term goal – the goal for that particular session. So that goal may be 'to determine what options are available to me and some first action steps towards making them happen'[17]. We are separating out the *topic* (fitness), the *longer-term aspiration* or *end goal* (to run the London marathon in six months' time in under four hours) and the goal for the session itself. And, just as importantly, we're helping generate in our coachee some awareness of the parameters of the issue and the responsibility for making it happen.

useful Goal-related questions

- How do you think I can help you?
- What would you like to leave this meeting with?
- What would success look like to you?
- What would you like to be different at the end of this conversation?
- Is that possible in the time we have together?
- What is the end goal you have in mind?
- How can we make that more specific?
- When would you like to achieve this by?
- How reasonable or attainable is this end goal?
- How will you know when you have achieved your goal?
- How would you measure progress along the way?
- What is the ultimate purpose?

R is for Reality

This is essentially the data gathering and questioning part. In my 'I want to get fitter' example, most of the coaching questions ('What's your diet like?', 'How much weight do you want to lose?' and so on) are checking out the current reality as I see it. By asking the questions (and using periodic summaries and paraphrasing) you're raising my awareness of where I am now in terms of my fitness[18].

17 Such as where to source a badger costume.

18 A note on process is helpful here. It's rare that coachees, or members of your team who want to discuss a problem with you, know precisely what goal(s) they want to achieve. Your early attempts to help them come up with a SMART objective or well-formed outcome may be a little premature; experience has shown me that sometimes it's best to start with some Reality-style conversation, then go back to clarifying Goals and then continue with the Reality stuff. It's always important to go back to Goal, though, as this helps with the responsibility element.

An example of this is if I had a very blinkered view of fitness. I may be so focused on what sports I want to start so as to get fitter that I haven't even considered that diet may be part of a solution. But a coach does not say 'Have you considered dieting?' or 'You'll need to watch what you eat' – these are suggestions. You need to be in coaching mode, not telling mode. In coaching mode you'll ask me to describe my diet; bringing this aspect into focus in this way means I'm far more likely to consider it, because it gets round my natural defences to suggestions[19].

So the role of the Reality section is to use questioning and the offering of feedback if appropriate to generate awareness of the situation as the coachee sees it – and to bring into focus any distortions or subjectivity that may be clouding the issue. In essence, the coach is acting as the voice of reason, asking for descriptions, examples and evidence (as opposed to subjective opinions) to obtain an objective view of the situation for both parties. This is primarily where the not-so-dark art of Socratic questioning is used to its best advantage.

It's hard to remain impartial or non-judgemental at times. The job of the coach is certainly to challenge inconsistencies[20], generalisations and distortions of thinking, but not to evaluate them. Through your questioning you are forcing the coachee to think deeply and search for specific examples to enable them to make a thorough self assessment of their current reality.

When you spend most of your time in this part of the coaching conversation asking thoughtful, open questions that enable your coachee to add a structure to their random thoughts on the particular issue concerned, you're really helping to generate awareness. Your judgement needs to be reserved for monitoring the conversation to ensure that it's following an illuminating path. When we speak our answers to questions aloud, we engage more parts of the brain than if we just think them; it appears that this increases neural activity and connections and makes recall more likely.

Questions may be based around *actions or behaviours* ('When did that last happen? How often does it happen? What did you do in response?'), *assumptions* ('How do you know that it happened like that? How do you know that is true?'), *thoughts and opinions* ('What else is relevant? Why do you think that happened?') and *feelings* ('How did you feel about that? What are you feeling now? What do you notice about your emotional reactions?'). Many Reality-type questions are based on the standard interrogative ones – who, what, where, when, why and

19 Especially if it involves curbing the beer/kebab combo.

20 Perhaps between words and body language, or contradictory feelings/thoughts.

how. Try to limit the use of 'why' questions as they are often heard, if not actually meant, judgementally.

more useful Reality-related questions

- What actions have you taken so far?
- What were the results of trying that?
- Describe the current situation to me.
- Tell me more about that.
- Who else is involved?
- Who else needs to know?
- What is the impact on others?
- What are the consequences of that?
- What concerns you most about this?
- What has stopped you in the past?
- If you could wave a magic wand, what would the solution look like?
- Would it help if I told you what I've noticed?

Note that last question: as a line manager, it's your role to give feedback on performance and behaviours. Your feedback – or encouraging the coachee to think about feedback they've had before) is a useful part of the Reality stage of coaching if it's relevant to the goal/situation.

O is for Options

If the Goal and Reality have been thoroughly explored, then the next stage – the generation of options – starts to happen naturally. There is no evaluation at this point; the aim is to generate as many possible solutions or courses of action as possible. Applying the rules of brainstorming (see page 176) is useful here – getting the creativity going by listing as many options as possible without critiquing them, no matter how wacky.

It's vital that the generation of options is led by the coachee. Your job as coach is to draw them out – and the more thoroughly you have explored the current Reality, the easier this will be. This may involve asking some 'what if' questions if there are obvious blockages to creativity[21]. Only after you've generated a healthy list of options together do you evaluate them in terms of the advantages, disadvantages and limiting factors that you've identified.

---

21 Such as 'What if money was no object? What if that obstacle was removed?'

And only after such a list has been generated and you've tried to squeeze every last option out of your coachee should you as coach offer your own options to add[22]. This is often one of the hardest things to do when trying out a coaching approach to management. For a start, the coachee will probably expect you to have the answer and may not understand why you won't give it. Stay firm and trust the process![23] And let go of your own ego, too; your suggestions should carry the same weight as the coachee's.

The end point, then, is to have a (preferably written down) list of options, with clearly identified pros and cons attached to them.

useful Options-related questions

- What could you do to solve the problem?
- What else?
- What else?
- What else?
- What if money was no object?
- What would you really like to do if you could?
- What have you seen work elsewhere?
- What are the advantages and disadvantages of that?
- On a scale of 1–10, how would you rate that one?
- Would you like a suggestion from me?

W is for Wrap up

This is the bit that stops it being just a nice cosy chat and where things get decided. In this end part of the conversation, we're encouraging – even demanding – our coachee to choose between the options we've generated and to start identifying action steps to ensure there is a behavioural impact.

So we're not just asking them to choose; we're getting their commitment to action and clarifying the first of these actions with behaviours, milestones and acknowledgement of any support needed. When we realise that *we* are making the choice (becoming aware that we're responsible for our choices and that we *have* choices) the feeling of control reduces our emotional arousal and increases positivity.

---

22 I always ask permission: 'Would it be helpful if I shared one that's occurred to me?'

23 It's probably best not to say 'It's for your own good' or – even worse – 'You'll thank me when you're older'.

Here it's important to use language that assumes action. Avoid the 'What are you going to *try* to do' as this feels like you're letting the coachee off the hook. The atmosphere here should be one of quiet urgency: what are they going to do and by when?

Usually there are a few options chosen that will work together. Once these are chosen by the coachee, agree timescales for the first steps, being as specific as possible. Ensure that any actions are relevant to achieving the goal and that any support/permissions/notifications are identified. Now is a good time to prompt the coachee into identifying things that may block progress towards meeting the goal; you can help them to think in advance how the effects of these may be mitigated.

So the coachee leaves the session with an action plan that they have come up with through your facilitation skills. There are actions, dates, identification of possible obstacles, clarity of support required and more than all that, a learning process – both parties have learnt from the discussion.

There should also be a palpable commitment to carrying out the actions agreed. Some coaches ask for their commitment on a 1–10 scale; if the answer is low, put the ball back in the coachee's court by asking 'What would get your commitment to a 10?'

some useful Wrap-up-related questions

- What are you going to choose out of these options you have identified?
- What are the first steps going to be?
- When are you going to do them?
- How do these actions meet your original goal?
- How will you know when you have succeeded?
- What support do you need?
- What might prevent you from achieving these actions?
- What can you put in place to prevent these obstacles?
- What else might need to be considered?
- On a 1–10 scale, how committed are you to carrying out these actions by the timeframe you agreed?
- What might get that figure higher?

Of course not every coaching-style conversation is prompted by a member of your staff knocking on your door and saying 'Can you help me with this problem?'[24] Sometimes there's a performance problem to discuss, and though this is a line management issue, a coaching approach is often the most effective way to address it.

Getting from where an individual is in terms of their performance to where they want to be (their goal) requires having to determine these two positions – i.e. the goal, and a thorough assessment of where they are currently in terms of their performance. Without this assessment, the aspects of performance the coachee is trying to address can be intangible and woolly, and while you may have ideas (and concrete feedback) of what needs to be improved, when you act as performance coach your approach is to help the coachee to determine what specific aspects of their performance need improving, and what they (and you) want it to look like.

In determining these criteria, an appreciative enquiry approach (see Chapter 20) may be more motivational for the coachee. This involves determining what they currently do well, what pleases them about specific aspects of their performance, identifying successes, describing how they're feeling and what they're thinking when having a good day, and getting the coachee to rate these aspects of their performance on a 1–10 scale.

objectivity

We've seen above that one of the crucial aspects of examining a coachee's current Reality is objectivity. Objectivity is affected by distortions such as opinions, judgements, desires and prejudices, and your key role as coach in this aspect of the GROW model is to help the coachee bypass potential distortions and determine as close to an objective reality as possible.

This is done through the use of descriptive terminology (detailed, specific) as opposed to evaluative terminology. Most 'normal' conversation is peppered with judgements such as good, bad, failure, success and vague or fuzzy generalisations. If you're merely being a 'line manager addressing a performance issue' then the major problem here may be defensiveness; taking a coaching approach is more likely to get to the crux of the issue.

Determining such objective, clear and specific performance assessment data can also lead to discussions and insights into what's currently holding

24 Although it's amazing how quickly your coaching fame will spread ...

the coachee back from improving on these specific criteria. The act of determining tangible measures can lead to a more ready examination of blocks to improvement and strategies for addressing them. Finally, it can help provide clearer monitoring in the future by helping the coachee to determine how performance has improved in observable, measurable terms.

perfectionism

One further point is relevant here when talking about performance assessment. As a line manager, you'll have your own ideas about performance levels required and can feed these in to a coaching conversation during the Reality stage of the GROW model. Coachees will also have their own ideas – and one coaching issue in a managerial context that often rears its head is one not of poor performance per se, but one of perfectionism[25].

While the drive for high standards can be generally regarded as a positive thing, the drive for perfectionism takes this desire to an unhealthy or at least unhelpful degree. The drive for excessively high standards may lead to misdirected priorities – a person may attempt to achieve perfection on one project at the expense of other aspects of their work that also need attention. They may also be continually dissatisfied with their performance or outputs, irrespective of whether they have actually achieved success in their work.

This can have a destructive effect on mood, energy and confidence levels – in their minds, nothing they do quite hits the mark and therefore they are not allowing themselves the satisfaction of a job well done or achieving any positive reinforcement. Those very definitions of success or what good performance itself looks like may be unrealistic or skewed, further perpetuating the problem.

While it does depend on what's driving the perfectionist tendencies, if the person is being driven by a fear of failure leading to rejection, criticism or disapproval, this can become a rather circular and reinforcing process. The person strives for something unattainable to avoid the rejection or criticism, and when they inevitably don't meet their own high standards this reinforces the sense of failure. This may lead to emotional disturbance and high levels of anxiety before, during and after the performance.

---

25 If I had a pound for every time I've heard a manager say they wish they had this problem with their staff, I'd have about £7. Anyway, it can be a very real and distressing problem for people and can lead to poor (or no) decision making and stress related illnesses.

There are other by-products of perfectionist tendencies. Constant striving for perfection may lead to a tendency to avoid closing down on ideas or projects so that things are left undone. Decisions can be deferred or avoided altogether, resulting in a tendency to procrastinate.

Perfectionism can also lead to an unhealthy fear of the competition, with the person becoming overly self critical and intolerant of their own or others' mistakes. It may also result in a tendency to avoid reviewing performance in terms of what can be learnt from it; if a person can't identify what went well with a piece of work, they may lose transferable learnings. Finally, a major peril of perfectionism is a very simple one; a person with this tendency may be unable to derive any pleasure at all from their labours, resulting in constant lowered mood states, generalised anxiety or even depression.

how to help

As a manager/coach, you can help your staff with clarity on what constitutes excellent performance (as opposed to perfect performance) and help ensure that such efforts are channelled into the right areas. You're helping provide a sanity check.

By having clear, structured conversations with staff members you suspect of having perfectionist tendencies and providing honest, constructive feedback, you're also making such efforts sustainable in the long term – and helping such individuals see failures and setbacks as opportunities for learning, not self condemnation. You may also be potentially saving your organisation from a stress at work claim!

benefits of using the GROW approach

The beauty of the GROW approach is that it's simple and intuitive to use, while being very effective. Whether you use it to address performance concerns, or general problem solving/ideas generation, a coaching approach to managerial conversations punches above its weight.

Coaching fulfils the major components of empowerment (generating responsibility, trust, development and support) and improves your own conversational, managerial and organisational skills at the same time. Together with goal setting and the giving of constructive feedback, these skills, easily learned with practice, are the beating heart of the Psychological Manager.

chapter 14

will and motivation

So far in this section we've dealt with the skill part of the skill/will matrix. But skill is only half the story. Two people can have identical intellect, personality styles and preferences, and knowledge, skills and experience, but very different levels of performance will result if one is motivated and the other isn't.

So this chapter deals with the *will* – motivation and attitude. We've looked at the world of motivation in theoretical form, and this section explores what you as a manager can do about it.

Motivation is something you as a manager have to do something with; it's a 'doing' word. Most managers don't; but you – as a Psychological Manager– are different.

the psychological contract

Before we look more closely at motivation, a word on the psychological contract. Much has been written about this over the last 50 years[1], but very little about what

1 I suggest you don't go and read it.

you as a manager need to know about it and, more importantly, how it impacts on your management of people[2]. Every writer seems to have their own definition, but most come down to the following few core essentials. A psychological contract, as distinct from the formal employment contract, is generally:

- unwritten, subjective and ongoing
- shaped by the organisation but held by individuals
- comprised of all the beliefs an individual holds about that organisation.

Many of these beliefs are connected with a sense of equity or fairness, and as such can have a powerful impact on behaviour. These beliefs can change over time and will vary between individuals depending on their own backgrounds, motivations and aspirations.

As the psychological contract is by its very nature subjective, its contents will vary from individual to individual. One employee in your team may have the adequate provision of development opportunities as part of their unspoken contract; others may have promotional expectations as part of theirs and yet others may be more focused on personal welfare and security of employment. The main point is that the psychological contract is about *exchange*; the employee exchanges their labour and goodwill for a set of implicit expectations around such issues of promotion, development, respect and fairness.

You'll notice one recurrent theme here; this contract is all inside people's heads. Its implicit nature means that it's generally hidden, not written down anywhere, and you often don't know what an individual's psychological contract contains until it's been breached.

This happens all the time, apparently, because of all the factors that affect the employment relationship. Many are accidental, intangible and formed of a subjective evaluation of what's been promised (or what's expected) and what's actually transpired.

The implications of such a breach are varied: there may be an impact on feelings (anger, betrayal, sadness), thoughts ('I'm not going to go the extra mile now'; 'What's the point in being loyal?') and, ultimately, actions (less effort, work to rule, active retaliation by taking more sick leave or leaving early). We're back to equity theory again (see page 80); a perceived breach of the psychological contract will meet with reduced effort so as to achieve balance in the exchange[3].

2 That's why.

3 Actually, the research suggests that such a breach has a big impact on attitudes, but rather less on behaviour.

what you can do

While this is all very interesting, what can you do about it? That last sentence is indicative, actually; in a survey, 90% of organisations said the psychological contract was a useful concept, but only 36% of them actually used it[4]. The answer – you've guessed it – is to have good old fashioned conversations with your staff.

The more you make the implicit explicit, the more both you and your team members will benefit. Through regular, open and honest conversations, you can explore hitherto unspoken desires, aspirations and expectations and ensure that they are not breached by default because you didn't know about them and the employee hadn't crystallised them.

The sooner you can start doing this after selection, the better. Some organisations attempt to address this during recruitment and induction; in any event, start soon and ensure that this concept becomes a regular topic in your routine review meetings. Remember – although a psychological contract is between an employee and the organisation, on most practical levels when you're a line manager, the organisation is *you*.

To have a positive effect (or at least avoid a negative one) then any promises you make as part of these discussions must be made genuinely and followed through. If there's one thing worse than breaching an aspect of the psychological contract that you weren't aware of, it's breaking one that you were aware of.

One thing to avoid, however, is the tit-for-tat bargaining that can sometimes accompany this. A give-and-take relationship is healthy, while one that habitually descends into explicitly contracting some extra effort for a specific reward becomes prescriptive, inflexible and controlling.

motivation conversations

The psychological contract can obviously have a big impact on motivation. But since it's not always explicit or known to all parties, how are you going to know what motivates the individuals whom you manage? I'll give some specific ideas at the end of this chapter, but for now let's start with the obvious.

The answer again comes down initially to one thing: quality conversations. If you want to know what drives someone, ask them. OK, it's not always as simple as that, but it's a good start. Through your one-to-one sessions, you should start to gain an impression of what it is (either internal to them, or in the job itself) that

4 Guest & Conway (2002) in Conway and Briner (2005).

keeps that person motivated. The idea here is to start making this specific and tangible, as opposed to it merely floating in the ether.

Of course it's not always that easy. Some people have never been asked this question before. One individual I managed in a public sector organisation was used to being told what to do (and how to do it), irrespective of that individual's experience, personality or indeed ability, not to mention any longer-term aspirations. My well meaning but clumsy attempts to try to understand how I could make the job more rewarding for her, or more suited to her style and experience, was met at first with suspicion, followed by gentle mirth[5], and eventually fear and frustration[6].

So part of the answer here is about you creating the right environment, atmosphere and culture where these sorts of questions are asked, and meaningful answers routinely given. It takes time to build up the trust (in some places far more than others), but ultimately this is one of the things that you have control over. You can make a real difference to the way people do their jobs.

Merely coming out with a 'What motivates you?' type question, however, may not help you much. Most of us don't know what motivates us – or at least haven't given it any structured thought. The question is too abstract and needs a framework.

This is where modern motivation questionnaires come in; they get at these answers through the back door, as it were, and add a useful framework to the conversation. You don't need to use the questionnaire approach, of course (you have to be a qualified user for some of them), but these questionnaires have distilled the research into a framework of (usually between nine and eleven) motivating factors that typically float boats.

One such questionnaire and supporting motivation framework is the Blue Edge Motivation Questionnaire (BEM-Q ©[7]). The model they use assesses 11 factors that can be either motivators or demotivators (by their absence) at work. These are:

- **Affiliation**: a desire to work closely with other people, getting to know them and being at the centre of social events.
- **Recognition**: a desire for acknowledgement for their efforts and receiving positive feedback from others.

---

5 'Yeah, we don't do this around here. You'll learn.'

6 'Why won't you just tell me what you want me to do and leave my opinions out of it?'

7 Other excellent motivation questionnaires are available [*Legal Ed*].

- **Caring**: a desire to nurture others in the work role and being seen as a 'shoulder to cry on' by others.
- **Independence**: a desire to work autonomously without the heavy involvement of superiors, valuing personal freedom.
- **Development**: a desire for ongoing personal and professional development through training, coaching and other learning opportunities.
- **Responsibility**: a desire to take positions of responsibility and influence over others, valuing the status associated with those more senior positions.
- **Achievement**: a desire to set and achieve stretching goals, being recognised for achieving them.
- **Variety**: a desire to do original, creative, interesting work, valuing work environments which encourage innovation.
- **Material**: a desire to make money and achieve a good remunerative package.
- **Security**: a desire to work in a secure and stable role and organisation; more likely than most to believe in the 'job for life' model.
- **Environment**: a desire to be happy and comfortable in the physical working environment.

Here you'll recognise some key components of the theories from earlier chapters: for example, *Affiliation* relates to Maslow's concept of social needs, *Security* with safety needs, and *Material* with Herzberg's hygiene factors. The factors that Herzberg claimed enriched the job (as opposed to merely enlarge it) are there, too – Independence, Responsibility, Variety and Recognition. While the factors that motivate us are more transient than, say personality preferences, general themes do emerge, and identifying the top three motivating factors with your staff, and assessing the extent to which their current role meets these needs, is very useful information.

Once you know what these motivating factors are (and if you don't go down the questionnaire route, you can always use the above as a structure for a conversation) then you can work with your team to ensure as far as you can that their job provides some scope for satisfying these needs. Remember, this is letting you know when they are operating at their best, so you may need to ask them to describe specific circumstances when they were particularly fired up and working well, and what contributed to that feeling.

It's also useful to find out when each individual felt at their most demotivated and what that meant in terms of their work performance – and again, what it was about the circumstances that contributed to it. Another useful question you could ask is 'If you were your manager, what would you do to get the best out of you?'

If an individual has a strong preference for Achievement, for example, then what can you do to ensure that they are actively involved in the setting of their own goals? What can you do to help make these goals stretching in the context of organisational needs? How can you ensure that the individual gets adequate recognition for meeting those stretching goals? How can you link this with advancement opportunities?

Of course not everything is within your gift[8]. A useful approach is to discuss the extent to which the job as it stands satisfies the person's top three motivating factors, and to get them to come up with suggestions for how the job may be enhanced accordingly. As manager, it's your job to meet these ideas as far as you can while meeting your own requirements for that role. This may involve adjusting your management style accordingly – for example, delegating more responsibility, allowing more autonomy in the way they perform tasks, using more coaching-style conversations and the like.

By doing this you're using the skill/will matrix at its best, and behaving like a true theory Y subscribing manager. These conversations may also touch on the 'when' of motivation, as opposed to the 'what'. Be alert to any perceptions of inequity, or of behavioural choices linked to expectations, to help you to address them before they have a deleterious effect on performance.

leadership style

All of this is at the heart of the Situational Leadership © model: you are adjusting your style to tap into what makes the different individuals in your team perform at their optimum. You'll have to take different approaches, at different times, with different people. You'll also have to ensure that you reward the behaviours – and performance – that you want, and that your team see the link between the performance and the reward. And what motivation theory tells us is that for most people, most of the time, it's not about the money.

We'll now look at *what* you do *when* – how you use your assessment of skill and will in a particular circumstance to determine your leadership style. Situational Leadership is about varying your style of management based on your

8 At the time of writing, not many managers can give many security need assurances ...

judgement of an individual's skill and will to do a task. As we discussed on pages 86–87, there are four possible scenarios:

- both a **low current ability** to perform the task and a **low desire** to do so
- a **low current ability** to perform the task but **motivated and willing**
- a **high level of skill** or potential to perform the task but **unwilling**
- a **high level of skill** or potential and **motivated and willing** to do so.

Let's take these scenarios one at a time and identify what predominant style of leadership you should display to get the best performance out of the individual concerned.

low skill, low will

Nothing's going to happen until you deal with the motivation issue. So – if you haven't done this already – the first stage is to have a conversation about the employee's wider aspirations and how this particular task taps into what typically motivates them.

You may be able to adjust the task so that it meets these primary motivators. For example, if they have a strong need for affiliation/working with others, can you encourage some joint working on aspects of the task? If they're motivated by recognition, how can you build this in and make it publicly noted? You may also wish to reiterate how important the piece of work (and therefore their performance) is towards meeting the goals and objectives of the team.

Once you have at least a modicum of buy-in (or at least agreement that they'll take the work on) you can build on the skill. Initially, your approach in this scenario is a directive one, clearly setting out the objectives of the piece of work, what it involves and any key stages and milestones. Clarity is the key here – make everything obvious, tangible and unambiguous. Make any goals SMART and make sure they know what excellent performance looks like.

As the work progresses, use a pretty hands-on style. Help them to structure the task, set deadlines and make it clear what they should be reporting back to you on and by when. Build motivation by acknowledging successes, giving regular feedback and praising when appropriate. Monitor performance regularly and deal with any problems or breaches of standards by providing instant feedback and reiteration of what performance standards are expected. Help them to identify any training or development needs that can improve their performance or knowledge.

This directive style may go against your preferred or natural style of leadership, but it's important to recognise that if the individual has low skill and (at least initially) low will to perform this task, then they'll probably lack confidence in performing it and don't want to be left to work alone.

The more time and support you can give at the start of the process will pay dividends in skill improvement through your goal setting and feedback (and perhaps gentle and increasing forays into coaching). Motivation and confidence should rise, too, through your feedback and praise. Eventually, and hopefully in subsequent tasks, you'll be able to use a different style.

low skill, high will

In both scenarios 2 and 3, your coaching skills will come to the fore – albeit for different reasons. In scenario 2, the motivation element is not the problem, so if skill/experience is very low for a particular task, an initial directive approach as in scenario 1 is often appropriate.

You may, however, be able to drop this fairly quickly and take advantage of the high will by using a coaching and guiding style. As with all coaching interventions, creating an atmosphere of trust – and one where mistakes are tolerated and viewed as learning experiences – is paramount. As confidence and skill levels rise through your initial 'hand-holding'[9] you'll gradually be able to let go of the control and put increasing responsibility for decisions on the employee[10].

high skill, low will

For this scenario use primarily a coaching style of intervention, but one that focuses on increasing motivation as opposed to working on skills. Your coaching approach needs to address the reasons behind the low motivation, identifying any blockages to the realisation of performance potential that are already there, and using your knowledge of motivation theory to find ways round these blockages.

This is usually through a combination of working on the person (perhaps by looking at their perceptions of the task and helping them with reframing), and if possible tailoring the task so it better meets their motivational needs or preferences.

---

9 Concentrating on the holy trinity of goal setting, feedback and coaching.

10 *The One Minute Manager* series by Ken Blanchard takes quite a 'controlling' view of coaching in any event. It's sometimes a subtle distinction, but he puts coaching in the 'Directive Behaviour' bracket, which wouldn't sit well with many coaches.

It may well be the case that what you thought was a motivational issue is actually a confidence issue; if this is the case, you can help by encouraging small but increasing steps, giving plenty of feedback (searching for opportunities to praise) and reinforcing this through awareness and responsibility-inducing coaching conversations. Supporting and firing up the person are the principal concepts here.

high skill, high will

It's easy to assume that you don't have to do anything with this scenario, but don't fall into the trap of being an absent manager![11] There's a fine line between giving highly able and motivated people the freedom and responsibilities to perform their tasks with minimal supervision, and merely ignoring them and letting them get on with it.

To maintain motivation it's still essential to give feedback and praise. Using the strengths approach – identifying what they are doing well and how this can be translated into other aspects of work – will not only maintain motivation, but the resulting creativity may also lead to the meeting of fresh goals and challenges that were hitherto unthought-of.

Of course in this scenario it's unlikely that you'll have to closely monitor the way in which the objectives are being met. Although setting goals and objectives is just as important as in the other scenarios, you can allow far more freedom as to how the objectives are met. You can probably allow more risks, too[12]. Your coaching, when it's needed, will be very much from the 'exploring options and realising potential/increasing creativity' perspective, and will be largely led by the coachee.

When managing talented people like this (or at least talented on this particular task), good delegation practice is important. Are you delegating both power *and* responsibility? What is the scope in terms of decision making powers? Have you made it clear how the task fits in with the bigger picture? Have you ensured there are enough resources available? And what level of reporting progress back needs to be agreed? If you make all this explicit up front during the goal setting conversation, it will be easier for both of you.

---

11 Some managers believe that managing 'talent' is harder than managing poor performers, often because there's the underlying feeling that they are after your job ...

12 But please, not if you're in the financial sector. We don't want *that* again.

sections three and four checklist

So that's it – the skill/will matrix and what to do with it. It's likely that you're already doing most of it intuitively, but being more aware of the framework and the particular leadership styles you can use, depending on the scenario you have in front of you, can only be a good thing. Unless, of course, you're Brian Clough[13].

the psychological manager:

- Role-models the behaviours they wish to see in others and creates a culture of conversation.
- Uses the skill/will matrix to firstly assess, then help to build the skill and the will of their staff.
- Varies their management style according to individual and situational need and is comfortable using all those styles.
- Is aware of how individuals differ – intelligence, personality, beliefs, attitudes and knowledge, and motivation – and has a broad understanding of these concepts and the major theories involved.
- Takes a proactive approach to motivation, recognising that everybody is motivated by different things at different times.
- Helps their team members to define clear goals and objectives that are SMART and tap into the wider vision of the team, and have regular conversations about progress on those goals.
- Aligns performance goals with personal development goals to foster commitment and motivation.
- Sets up systems to facilitate the constructive, regular feedback against goals and behaviours with all their staff and creates and role-models a culture where this is the norm.
- Takes a coaching approach to their management practice, regularly practising and honing their coaching skills and getting feedback on their coaching interventions.
- Is aware of the concept of the psychological contract and, as in more general motivational drivers, makes an effort to make it explicit.

---

13 My final Brian Clough quote: 'They tell me people have always wondered how I did it. That fellow professionals and public alike have been fascinated and puzzled and intrigued by the Clough managerial methods and technique and would love to know my secret. I've got news for them. So would I.'

section

five

building your team:

understanding and managing

teams as separate entities

This section shifts the focus away from the individuals within your team, and on to the team itself.

As a manager of a group of people, you are responsible not only for each individual's performance against the goals you've set with them, but also for those individuals' development opportunities. You are also responsible (and no doubt accountable) for the performance and development of the team as a construct in itself[1]. As a Psychological Manager, your aim is to balance the interests of the individuals in your team and the interests of the team as a whole[2].

To most of you, precisely who your team is will be obvious; usually the people who report to you to perform the work of the department you lead. There may also be cross-functional teams – those drafted in from various parts of the organisation (or even across organisations) to perform a particular task or project. These individuals may have their own bosses, with a different, specified manager for the particular task in hand. This can add a different level of complexity (and calls for good communication between all parties) but the principle is the same; the team, or group (from now on I'll use these terms interchangeably), has its own identity separate from those of its individual members, and is something that needs to be actively managed.

This is the central point here (and the lack of which I've noticed time and time again in many organisations). Managers often focus on the task at hand, and at a push will manage the performance and development of the members of their team. However, they often pay scant attention to group processes such as team identity, communication, conflict resolution and problem solving[3].

A team is therefore a separate entity from its collection of individuals. When the group processes are working as well as they can, the team will become greater than the sum of its parts. When they are not, performance can drop to below the level of all the individuals. Many sports teams fail to reach their potential because the egos of individuals don't allow for being subsumed into the collective. The senior executive board that resorts to infighting and generally dysfunctional behaviour can cripple an organisation, irrespective of their individual talents[4].

---

1 You couldn't have a high-performing England football team if you took account only of the skills of the individuals within it and not the way they performed as a – oh.

2 And of course – going back to Section two – your own.

3 Please note: a once-a-year teambuilding day in the hands of a consultant is not enough. It's a good start, though. My contact details are at the back. Seriously, though, my point is that it's a constant maintenance thing, not a tickbox exercise when you have the budget.

4 I'm not writing from personal experience here, though. Definitely not.

chapter 15

about the team

groups and teams

group needs

Balancing the interests of the individuals in your team with the interests of the team itself is the major premise underpinning the ideas of John Adair. According to Adair, we bring three needs with us when we join a group, and these needs desire expression. As team leader, this can provide a useful framework to ensure you're keeping everything in balance:

- We bring with us our needs as an *individual*; to express them, to broaden our experience and to develop our skills.
- We need to be part of a *group*. This includes our desire for social identity (see Chapter 16) and the processes by which the group achieves what it sets out to achieve.
- Then there is the *task* itself – the content – of what the individuals and group as a whole are there to perform.

These three needs (usually depicted as three overlapping circles) do not work in isolation but rather are affected by the others. For example, accomplishing a meaningful task will satisfy the need of the individual who played a part in it and also the need of the group in achieving a sense of group cohesion and bond.

Your job as team leader is therefore to recognise your responsibility for these three components. Through managing and developing the individuals in your team, and building/maintaining the team identity and processes, the task gets done[1].

group identity

Groups, and the dynamics within them, have been the subject of social psychological research for many decades. The definitions of what makes a team need not concern us too much, as in the work context it's usually a given. Kurt Lewin was one of the first writers concerned with group identity, suggesting that it was the experience of a common fate that determined whether you saw yourself as part of a particular group or not (relevant to the need for group goals as we'll see later).

Lewin's work, in 1948, was influenced by his experiences in the Second World War; he argued that the Jews were a cross-border group by way of their common fate of stigmatisation and imprisonment. Sherif and Sherif (1969) were more concerned with the existence of some form of social structure, with clearly defined roles and relationships. The family is often quoted as an example here, but the concept again is relevant to the world of work as anyone who has been part of a work group will recognise[2].

stages of team development

Before we look at the world of group psychology, let's just examine what stages a team typically goes through during its development. Perhaps the classic model for how teams tend to develop over time is Tuckman's model from the 1960s (further developed in the 1970s), which in many ways parallels the

1 I've heard it said (by me mainly, but I'm sure I got it from somewhere) that once you're managing a reasonably-sized team (say ten or so), then you shouldn't really be doing much else. Your objectives and the objectives of the group and the individuals within it should be the same, so the 'day job' becomes one of full-time manager, as opposed to one of 'I manage a team when I get round to it/after I've finished my own work/when they make a bloody hash of it'.

2 If anything, definitions of groups have got simpler over the years. Rupert Brown (1988) came up with my favourite: a group exists because we say so and at least one other person does.

Situational Leadership model described in Chapter 14. You can use the two frameworks in tandem, varying your management style according not only to the individuals concerned but also where the team is in its formation.

Tuckman suggested that as a team grows in maturity it passes through distinct stages. Your general management style could and should vary according to these stages. The model assumes a team coming together for the first time – but similar effects are seen if a new manager is appointed; the first forming stage may start all over again.

forming

In this initial stage, the team members are unsure of where the team is going and their part in it. They look to the leader for clear guidance about goals, objectives and individual roles and responsibilities. There may be little discussion of personal matters, with a sense of 'false' politeness and individual reticence about putting themselves forward or owning up to skills/experience.

The manager is virtually obliged to use a directive style, dealing with concerns and uncertainties with as much clarity and guidance as possible. Regular team meetings and open discussions are welcomed by the team.

Run some 'getting to know you' sessions so that people start to connect on an interpersonal level; this can help to build trust and set the right tone. Try to establish a supportive, informal climate with some social activities if possible. Finally, ensure that all the members are aware of the group purpose and their role in it.

storming

In the second stage team members attempt to assert their rights and position within the team, establishing a pecking order of expertise and perceived seniority with each other and particularly with the leader. In this *storming* phase, the clarity of purpose for the team may have been addressed, but now individuals are more concerned with their own power struggles. This may also include those jockeying to be deliberately low profile.

The manager needs to assert their authority in dealing with any conflicts that have arisen, and a coaching style helps the team focus on goals, thereby diffusing any emotional concerns. It may be prudent to let some conflicts (such as defensiveness, competition, jealousy and animosities) play out as they are an essential element of maturing relationships[3].

---

3 Otherwise they just fester and turn up again when you least expect it.

You can help by reinforcing appropriate ways of dealing with the conflict; this has the added benefit of you being seen to assert your authority in a constructive manner. At times you may need to assert your authority and remind people what is and is not acceptable. This stage is often brief but can be highly charged: the motto is 'keep calm and carry on'. Celebrate successes when you can and ensure the success is seen as a team, not individual, effort.

norming

During the third stage it all starts to settle down into a form of consensus. In this *norming* phase, any roles, responsibilities and formal (or perceived) hierarchies have usually been negotiated and accepted and a sense of common purpose starts to prevail. There is also a building and acceptance of ground rules and norms of behaviour and working practices; systems are being set up and decisions are increasingly joint ones. Personal and interpersonal issues are now more likely to be discussed in an adult to adult manner.

The leader may find that a facilitative style helps to generate creativity and flexibility of thoughts and ideas, as well as confidence.

Build the skill and the will of the individuals within the team, and where possible increase personal responsibilities. As with all these stages, your actions as manager can reduce the time it takes to go through the phases and get to the last one. Trust the process and experiment!

performing

Finally[4], we're cooking on gas. In the final *performing* stage, the team is only now working at its most efficient, knowing what it's doing and why, and committing to a common purpose. A sense of autonomy starts to creep in.

The leader is able to take more and more of a delegative role, delegating both responsibility and power to individuals or the team/sub-groups as appropriate, giving rewards and feedback as appropriate and coaching when needed. The team now may be able to operate independently of the leader. Any disagreements and conflict situations that (inevitably) occur are dealt with constructively, often by the members themselves.

The team is able to deconstruct tasks by distinguishing between content (the *what*) and process (the *how*) in efforts to aid individual and team development. When this is working at its best, tasks themselves become learning interventions. As leader you should be encouraging, motivating and supporting, and – as we

4 Although Tuckman did add a later stage, *adjourning*, primarily because it rhymed.

mentioned at the start of this section – ensuring that you pay attention to both individual and team.

managing team development

Your job as manager, then, is to constantly take a healthcheck and review what stage your team has reached, and then how to facilitate moving to the next level. Be prepared for the team to slip back occasionally or even stagnate; this is not a failure but a natural reaction to events.

It will help if you constantly reinforce the behaviours you wish to see and refresh or even reinvent the end goals/purpose. And your biggest challenge is to be comfortable and competent in all the leadership styles and in knowing when to use them.

chapter 16

the psychology of groups

While any group is made up of the individual personalities and behaviours within it, research tells us that some fundamental psychological processes happen when those individuals become part of a group, so it's extremely useful to be aware of what typically happens when people work together.

The concept of the group has been scientifically studied for nearly 100 years, and we'll now look at the more well-known findings, which cover the fundamental principles underpinning group behaviour. Inevitably, this is not an exhaustive account, but provides a flavour of what you need to be aware of when leading your team.

While it's easy to assume that these processes are inevitable (which they usually are), this doesn't mean that the Psychological Manager can't have an influence; there is usually some variable you can control ...[1]

1 Nice Dan Brown-type ending there [*Ed*].

groups just happen: social interaction and social identity

Our sense of who we are, and our value to society, is inextricably linked to the social groups to which we belong. Maslow argued that our need for social interaction and belonging is halfway up our hierarchy of needs[2] and McClelland identified certain individuals who had a high need for affiliation (see Chapter 10). These theories reflect individual differences, but many have argued that the need to belong to a group is part of the human condition. This finds expression in our family groups, supporting a football team, being part of a music or cultural 'scene' and as being part of a team at work[3].

genes and neurons

For years evolutionary psychologists have talked about this as a survival strategy. As hunter-gatherers we were motivated to maintain mutually beneficial relationships to aid our survival. Richard Dawkins in *The Selfish Gene* argued that genes were not the only mechanism by which the essence of 'us' spreads; cultural and behavioural characteristics called memes (such as ideas and rituals) are spread between us in our social groups and evolve in the same way that genes evolve. Memes reproduce by social interactions because the groups that did so found an evolutionary advantage. While we are good replicators we're not perfect, and small twists and turns create a changing evolutionary path in our social behaviour in the same way as our genetic blueprint – albeit one that binds us socially together.

This idea has been further enriched by the recent work on mirror neurons. A large part of our modern brain is taken up with the hardware for social interaction because it was important for our past survival. It's as if we have the internal mechanisms for a kind of brain-powered social networking site helping us connect to others.

These connections are based on the ability to copy others' emotions and intentions; when we see someone purposely do something, the same area activates in our brains as if we had done the action ourselves. This is the

2 New research into mirror neurons suggests that it should be as basic a need to us as survival needs.

3 Studies of people who won the lottery show that many still go to work, or at least do voluntary work, for the meaning they derive from being part of a group and in contributing to something greater than themselves.

neurology behind empathy[4]; it helps us to react appropriately to others by understanding what they're feeling, and may be intending to do. It may be the reason why we learn effectively through imitation. Recent research has shown that even superficial feelings of 'connectedness' with a stranger are enough to lead to a mirroring of emotions and even heart rate[5]. When we connect with people in this way, we get a rush of feelgood chemicals that makes us want to do it more, and helps us get over our natural predisposition towards viewing others as a threat.

This process, then, explains why emotions tend to be contagious. Whenever we pick up a strong emotion from others, our mirror neurons light up and we start feeling the same thing. The effect is even more pronounced when it's the boss who's originating the emotion – another reason why you should be role-modelling the behaviours you wish to see from others.

social identity

So it's apparent that a large part of our learning comes from social interaction and that it fulfils an important need within us. Our brains appear to be hardwired to interact and respond to others, and as such the groups we are in form a large part of our social identity. Social identity theory tries to explain in behavioural terms why and how we form our social groups and how they affect our behaviour.

When we join a group, then, we're (re)defining who we are and making a statement about how we see ourselves and want to be seen by others. A group of people living in the same English town may see themselves primarily as northern, English, British or European – and that's without the added complexities of gender, religion, sexual preference or ethnic background.

Social identity is that element of our self image that comes from our 'choice' of group membership. The term was originally coined by Henri Tajfel and John Turner in the 1970s, and is based on the somewhat obvious premise that we prefer a positive to a negative self image – their contribution is that they made

4 It appears that autism may be a result of this system going wrong.

5 Cwir et al (2011) suggest that when we feel this sense of connectedness, however it comes about, we psychologically blur the boundary between self and others, leading to shared emotional and physiological states. If this can happen with strangers, the implications of your empathic mirroring with friends, family and work colleagues are obvious.

the link between our self image and the groups that we belong to (or are even randomly assigned to[6]).

As a consequence, we evaluate the groups that we're in (the in-group) more positively than those we aren't in (the out-group), often requiring initiation rites to ensure the 'exclusivity' of our in-group. We associate ourselves with the characteristics of the group – what Turner called self stereotyping – which makes us appear (and believe that we are) more similar to each other than we are to those outside. We therefore play up our similarities and play down our differences – and conversely play up our differences and play down our similarities with members of other groups. This has a profound effect on our tendency towards competition, conformity and obedience (see page 143)[7].

So why does this happen? Apart from the resulting improvements in, or at least maintenance of, self esteem (we feel better about ourselves if we put others down), Tajfel argued that this social categorisation into in-group and out-group is in effect a cognitive shortcut. It's a way of simplifying this complex world and reducing the amount of data we have to process in order to make decisions. To make sure we can discriminate quickly between these two categories we blur any differences within those categories and sharpen those differences between them. Whichever categorisation 'system' we use at the time (male/female, Chelsea/Fulham supporter, Swallows or Amazons) is the one that is most salient at that particular moment.

The consequences of this for workplace behaviour are quite profound. Unfortunately, the desire to integrate and identify with a work group or department may lead to prejudice and negative stereotyping of other groups or departments. These may be triggered by real or perceived threats (unlikely to be physical nowadays, unlike in hunter-gatherer times where this behaviour may well be rooted) to resources or status. We may even blame the out-group for events that were within our own control, since we're more likely to give

---

6 Tajfel et al (1971) found that merely assigning people into two random groups (whether they preferred paintings by either Klee or Kandinsky, or even on the toss of a coin) was sufficient to produce in-group biases in behaviour (favouritism and discrimination in the allocation of rewards). This became known as the minimal group paradigm; a perceived conflict of interest is not necessary for intergroup bias – or, indeed, conflict.

7 Perhaps the classic portrayal in both literature and film of social identity and in-group/out-group biases is *Lord of the Flies* by William Golding. No-one told those boys to get into groups – it just happened. And didn't end very well, to be honest.

members of our in-group the benefit of the doubt – attributing the cause to anyone but us. At the extreme, this may lead to scapegoating[8].

Another result of attempting to maintain our social identity is the tendency for competitive behaviour – particularly with the out-group but also within the in-group – to maintain status. The act of competing with other groups may lead to enhanced performance and therefore isn't necessarily a bad thing; just being observed or in the presence of others may lead to enhanced performance, whether within our own group or in front of other groups.

However, competition can also be destructive and result in a lack of collaboration, silo-working or even sabotage[9]. Rock[10] suggests that this is primarily because we view working with people we don't know as a threat – and we automatically categorise them as foe until we prove them otherwise. The trick, then, is to get to know people in the out-group, by increasing our knowledge of them and forming relationships with them.

some shine, some hide: social facilitation and social loafing

social facilitation

In what must be one of the first social psychology experiments, in the 1890s Norman Triplett discovered that cyclists raced faster when they were racing with other cyclists[11]. This effect was coined *social facilitation* by Floyd Allport in 1924

---

8 The Ancient Greeks used to send a beggar out into the wilderness as a response to natural disasters, presumably to appease the gods. The Old Testament bible (*Leviticus*) describes a goat being outcast into the desert to atone for the sins of the people in much the same way – the sins conveniently go with it. Someone who is scapegoated, therefore, is someone who is blameless but blamed anyway. Freud would argue that we are projecting our own fears, thoughts and feelings on to others because we don't want to own them ourselves. The point is the target is usually an easier one than the 'actual' one, and it doesn't even have to be a goat.

9 One organisation I worked in had a history of silo-working, where one department would hide what it was doing from other departments, even viewing them as the competition – more so, in fact, than other competitor organisations. Using the management competency of 'Collaborating across boundaries' was one attempt to stop this behaviour, with managers having to demonstrate how they were, in fact, doing so.

10 *Your Brain at Work* by David Rock (2009).

11 He supposed this was due to the effects of competition.

when he found similar effects with participants being asked to do multiplication tasks. The social facilitation effect is now generally considered to be one where we perform better in front of others on simple tasks, but worse in front of others on more complex ones.

So why does this happen? Robert Zajonc (1965) suggested that this was primarily a function of arousal, where the presence of others increases our arousal levels which facilitates our performance on well-practised, habitual tasks, but interfered with tasks involving reasoning. Interestingly, he found the same effect with cockroaches; they ran faster than normal through a simple maze in the presence of other cockroaches and slower than normal through a more difficult one[12].

Other explanations for this effect range from the act of – or more specifically the fear of – being evaluated, to the arousing effects of distractions causing cognitive overload (which matters less if the task is simple). Finally, and perhaps most obviously, some argue that it's just about our desire to impress by doing brilliantly on a simple task, but the same desire results in the fear of potential embarrassment when we don't perform on a harder one.

While the reasons behind the social facilitation effect are up for debate, most researchers acknowledge that the effect is real and replicated across most situations. This has implications for assigning work within your team; if the task is simple, you may get increased performance if the individual is 'encouraged' to perform the task in the presence of the rest of the team. If the task is more complex, reduce the potential for cognitive overload by allowing more individual preparation time before any public viewing!

social loafing

There's no doubt that some people shine when performing in front of others or taking part in group tasks, whether it's about showing off, a sense of competition, increasing our sense of status or merely enjoying working in a group. There's also no doubt that some use group work to take the opportunity to hide, or at least put in less effort than they would if they were performing the task alone. There's been consistent research showing that, as the size of a group

12 Don't try this at home unless you have a large mallet.

increases, some group members reduce their own efforts accordingly[13]. This effect is known as *social loafing* (Latane et al, 1979)[14].

Again, the research supporting this assertion started early. Max Ringelmann in 1913 found consistently that people pulled less hard on a rope when pulling with others as opposed to on their own; this became known as the 'free-rider' effect as Ringelmann hypothesised that this was due to the participants being aware that they weren't being individually evaluated. Latane et al agreed that the effect appeared to be about the reduction in social pressure, as individual efforts were not identifiable. And both the size and location of the group have an impact; the larger the group, and the more 'virtual' those groups are, the more pronounced the social loafing appears to be; again, social pressure (or lack of it) is cited as being responsible for the effect[15].

Other explanations apart from social pressure have been posited. Do we feel more powerless in groups? Do we feel that our efforts are not rewarded, noticed or make a difference? The 'sucker' hypothesis[16] would say that we don't want to be the one that puts in all the work, so we wait to see what others will do before we make too much effort.

So what can you as a Psychological Manager do about the social loafing phenomenon? The answer is to increase the identifiability of members within the group, increase personal responsibility and accountability, and pay attention to (and give feedback on) group processes. Dan Rothwell (2004) suggests three ways to help with this:

- assign each group member specific tasks within the group's objectives (and make them personally accountable)
- make sure those tasks are perceived as worthwhile
- as far as possible allow an element of choice in what tasks individuals perform within the overall group task.

---

13 This is particularly true in western cultures; in more 'collectivist' cultures such as in China this effect doesn't seem to occur.

14 Social loafing is about the psychological motivations of individuals when working within groups. This is not the same as the effect of groups generally failing to reach their potential because of the inability to utilise efficiently all the resources potentially available to them or of faulty processes (Steiner, 1972).

15 Chidambaram & Tung (2005).

16 Thompson (2003).

resistance is useless: social influence, obedience and conformity

Some of the most (in)famous psychological experiments can be categorised under this heading. They were not concerned with group performance per se but rather with the tendency for people to conform to group pressure, figures of authority or to expected roles within a group. This heading covers the rather murky (and at times ethically suspect) world of social influence – more specifically, conformity and obedience, by looking at three of the most notorious studies.

Conformity is at the heart of social influence. Most people don't want to stand out from the crowd or go against norms of society[17]. In some cultures this is pretty much the rule, not just the norm[18]; in western culture it tends to be viewed negatively, but of course the alternative to at least an element of conformity is anarchy.

Asch conformity experiments

One of the first and most famous experiments into conformity and social pressure was performed in the 1950s by Solomon Asch. Asch recruited participants to ostensibly perform a test of vision, asking them to compare the length of a line against other lines, everyday objects and the like. The participants performed the experiment as part of a group – unknown to them, all in on the act. The correct answers to the comparisons were deliberately obvious; what Asch was trying to determine was whether the participants would change their minds and ultimately agree with the rest of the group, even when the answer the group gave was obviously incorrect.

Each participant (this was replicated over a hundred times) was put into a group of around seven other 'participants', and whenever each comparison was made the group gave their verdicts out loud, with the real participant going last. There were usually 18 trials within each experiment.

Asch's hypothesis was that people would not tend to conform on something so obviously wrong, but he underestimated the power of social pressure. Only

17 There are many obvious exceptions to this rule, of course, but the thing is we hear about them precisely because they stand out. The billions of us who don't, become invisible.

18 There's a saying in Japan: 'The nail that sticks out is hammered down'. There's also a (probably apocryphal) tale about Gary Lineker, when playing football in Japan, being told to reduce his performance because he was making the rest of the players look bad.

25% did not conform on any trial; 75% therefore conformed at least once, 37% conformed most of the time and 5% conformed every time. The size of the group didn't appear to have any noticeable effect once it had reached a minimum of three other members. However, it took only one other group member to give the obvious answer for the conforming effect on the participant to diminish.

So our pressure to conform to the rest of the group – driven by our desire for social acceptance – can override our common sense. This has implications for decision making as we'll see on page 147. It means that you can ultimately reach better decisions by generating a culture where healthy debate and disagreement is not only tolerated but encouraged. There are techniques to help this in group settings in Chapter 20[19].

Milgram studies on obedience to authority figures

One of Asch's students was a certain Stanley Milgram. Milgram built on Asch's findings on group conformity and focused on the area of obedience to authority[20]. His studies were borne out of the post-war feeling that there was something different about German people in terms of their mutual sense of morality that could lead them to commit the Holocaust atrocities[21].

The premise of the series of experiments (from the participants' viewpoint) was about learning and memory. The participant played the role of teacher, and a learner was supposed to be learning pairs of words. If the learner got an answer wrong, the teacher had to give them an electric shock, of gradually increasing (15-volt increments) magnitude. As the shocks increased, the learner screamed and banged on the wall for the experiment to be stopped. Milgram told the participants to continue, using a series of scripted prompts (i.e. 'The experiment requires that you continue'; 'You have no other choice, you must go on') and halted the experiment only if the participant still wanted to stop after all four prompts had been issued.

Of course the learners, like in the Asch studies, were in on the act and faking it, though the participant playing the part of the teacher didn't know this. So these participants believed that the learners were getting shocks of up to 450 volts, with the range of switches being labelled from 'Slight shock' to 'Danger – severe shock'. The final two were simply labelled 'XXX'.

---

19 For example, Edward De Bono's *Six Thinking Hats* technique (see page 178).

20 Strictly speaking, Milgram's work is more concerned with individual obedience rather than any group effect, but the implications of his work for a team leader will become obvious.

21 The research question 'Germans are different' probably wouldn't get through an ethics committee these days. In fact, Milgram's experiments wouldn't, as we shall see ...

In the first studies, a shocking[22] 65% of the participants went all the way to 450 volts, even while protesting and offering to refund the money they were paid. Milgram concluded that when people are commanded by an authority figure (he was performing the experiment as a Yale Professor on the Yale campus) not many people had the internal will to resist the commands of that authority. Later studies showed that one factor which did have an impact on the results was the proximity of Milgram himself; if the instructions to carry on were relayed by telephone, the participants' obedience levels decreased (the percentage of participants willing to go to 450 volts went down to 20%).

This experiment has been replicated countless times, and has even made it into the entertainment arena[23]. No differences were found between men and women, or when they were held in different locations[24]. In a rather bizarre twist of the story, two researchers wondered whether the participants really suspected that the learners were faking it, so they replicated the set-up using a puppy and real electric shocks as they presumably couldn't get the dog to act. They found similar results, although interestingly, of the 26 participants (13 men, 13 women), the 6 who refused to go all the way were all men; all 13 women gave the maximum shock allowed.

It became obvious to Milgram that not being German wasn't enough; our propensity to conform to authority figures is a universal trait. He gave two interpretations:

- that we conform out of a lack of expertise to make decisions (in effect, outsourcing the decision to someone who looks like they should know what they're talking about)
- that we don't view ourselves responsible for our actions if commanded by authority figures.

So what does this have to do with you, the Psychological Manager? It's hard not to become moralistic on this one: you can choose to use your authority-powers for good or evil. Be aware that your team may not question what you

22 Sorry. Pun absolutely intended.

23 Derren Brown performed a replication of the Milgram studies in 2006 for Channel 4 (*The Heist*) and a version was incorporated into a documentary shown on French TV in March 2010 (*Le Jeu de la Mort*).

24 Obedience rates went down, but were still high, when the experiments were performed in a disused office block instead of the Yale campus.

ask them to perform; again, encourage healthy, constructive debate rather than blind obedience[25].

Zimbardo's Stanford prison experiment

The third in our unholy trinity is one that many people are aware of; the Stanford prison experiments of Philip Zimbardo. Like the other two researchers Zimbardo was looking at conformity, and like the Milgram studies, his work has recently been replicated on British television[26]. Zimbardo's take on conformity, however, was focused on conformity to roles rather than an authority figure. He also believed that behaviour tended to degenerate under crowd conditions due to a loss of identity, personal responsibility and reduced concern for social evaluation; a psychological state he called *deindividuation*.

In 1971, Zimbardo constructed a mock prison at Stanford University. Twenty-four psychologically healthy volunteer students were randomly assigned to be either guards or prisoners for a fortnight and given props (such as weapons, mirrored sunglasses, ankle chains) and uniforms. The guards were given a briefing of the ground rules (no violence, but to instil fear, boredom and disorientation) and the prisoners were arrested at their homes, strip-searched and transported to the mock prison.

The experiment had to be halted after just six days. The prisoners were becoming distressed, submissive and emotionally disturbed due to the harsh treatment of the guards who had become bullying, aggressive and punitive. They used physical exercise as punishment, beat the prisoners with fire extinguishers and refused to let some prisoners urinate or defecate. Some prisoners were forced to go nude and sleep on a concrete floor as punishment for misdemeanours.

Zimbardo argued that both guards and prisoners had internalised their respective roles after this short period and seemed to want to carry on with the experiment. Even when payment stopped, the prisoners appeared to have accepted their lot and stayed where they were, reminiscent of the *learned helplessness* model of depression discussed on page 24. He suggested that the 'legitimising authority' and realistic setting had created the behaviour of both guards and prisoners (as opposed to any underlying personality traits of the individuals concerned) in a similar vein to the Milgram studies. Even Zimbardo

25 And never ask them to give anyone an electric shock. And keep the women away from puppies.

26 BBC Television's *The Experiment*, broadcast in 2002. The BBC's version is now taught on the UK A level syllabus.

himself accepted that he wasn't immune; as prison superintendent he permitted the abuse to continue.

Somewhat obviously, there have been ethical and methodological criticisms of this study, despite it being originally cleared by the American Psychological Association. Its generalisability to real life has also been questioned. However, some commentators have recently noticed the similarity between the Stanford prison and Abu Ghraib in Iraq. Along with the Asch and Milgram studies, there is a clear body of evidence that when we're in group situations, or in front of an authority figure, our capacity for obedience and conformity is far greater than is considered comfortable by most.

beware the risky shift: group polarisation and Groupthink

It's very easy to assume that the more people in a group there are to make a decision, the better that decision will be. After all, two (or more) heads are better than one. There is a wider range of expertise and experience, more people to ask questions and more people to challenge opinions.

Or conversely, maybe too many cooks spoil the broth? Does this just make the decision making process unwieldy and time consuming, resulting in paralysis by analysis? Or maybe the group decision is merely the average of all the individual positions[27]? While this may smack of compromise, it's certainly democratic.

Surprisingly, research shows us the answer is none of the above.

Stoner's study on group decision making

The classic study into group decision making was undertaken as part of an unpublished Masters thesis by James Stoner in 1961. Stoner randomly assigned participants into groups and asked them to make group decisions on hypothetical social situations, having first asked them to make individual ones

27 One fun teambuilding activity I've used is the desert survival one, where items salvaged from a plane crash in the desert have to be rank-ordered in terms of their usefulness for survival. The individuals in the group do a rank-order first, then they have to come up with a group answer – we then compare the two. Because there is a right answer (at least according to a Ray Mears-type expert) then the rankings can be compared numerically in how far the individual and the group scores differ from the correct one. The groups that work most effectively often have a score that's better than the average of the individuals; usually, however, this is not the case.

for comparison. These social situations usually involved choosing between two alternatives, one riskier than the other – for example, whether someone should trade salary for job security.

Stoner found that in the vast majority of trials, the group made riskier decisions than the average of the individuals within that group. This became known as the *risky shift phenomenon*, and the premise of the original study has been replicated countless times. Later refinements of these studies found that the group decision was not always riskier per se, but did tend to be more extreme. Group decisions tend to be riskier than the average of the individuals if those individuals made initial risky decisions on their own, and more cautious if they initially made cautious ones.

So the more extreme individuals are to begin with, the more extreme they tend to become when making decisions in a group. This tendency of group decisions to travel towards either end of the spectrum became known as *group polarisation*[28]. It appears that the act of discussion may prompt individuals to become more extreme to get their point across in a group setting, thereby strengthening the group's attitude.

There are serious implications of this, such as jury deliberations[29], public policy setting and executive boards – not to mention bullying on social media[30]. And the research supporting the idea continues to roll in; Luhan, Kocher and Sutter (2009) demonstrated that participants in groups were more selfish, competitive and less altruistic in their decision making than as individuals.

Why does this happen? After all, it is rather counter-intuitive! There are two main explanations for this polarising effect. Firstly, the *social comparison* explanation suggests that once we understand the rest of the group's position on the topic, we present ourselves and our views in the same direction to gain acceptance – but just that bit more extreme. The overall position therefore goes up a notch. The *persuasive argument* explanation takes the view that we weigh up the evidence for and against in such a decision-based discussion – but that weighing up is skewed in favour of the sheer volume of

---

28 Initially by Moscovici and Zavalloni in 1969.

29 Bray and Noble (1978) found that if a (mock) jury was initially predisposed to leniency, the result of the deliberations led to an even more lenient sentence – and the converse led to harsher penalties.

30 Research has shown that the polarising effect occurs over the internet, too ... (Sia et al (2002)).

information on the side of the majority. If we hear of new ways to support our own position, we argue more strongly for it[31].

This is not to say, of course, that a minority cannot influence the group decision[32]. It's just that it doesn't happen very often. When it does happen, it's often because that minority have been consistently independent (the same minority tending to disagree on various topics over a period of time) rather than merely being seen as reasonable or popular. Again, if you notice as manager that such polarisation of views can occur in your teams, then encouraging the constructive challenging of ideas may prevent the extremes – and may also prevent the other major decision making phenomenon that occurs in groups – Groupthink.

Groupthink

It should be apparent by now that most of us have a need for social inclusion and consensus, whether to help maintain our social identity or our tendency to conform to group pressure. When these needs get in the way of a thorough evaluation of the data, particularly in a tightly-knit, cohesive group[33], a sort of 'false consensus' occurs, with conflict, disagreement and suppressing of individual creativity.

If you add to the mix a strong, directive leader, time-pressures and poor decision making processes, then Groupthink can be the result; an increased desire for unanimity, an over-inflated sense that the group is right and the illusion that everyone has bought in to the solution. Anyone who does not agree becomes the 'out-group' and is told to quickly get back into line.

The seminal work on Groupthink was done by Irving Janis. His initial research was in analysing the foreign policy errors that had a disproportionate impact on the world stage, such as the Bay of Pigs situation in Cuba (in 1961, when the USA made a disastrous attempt to overthrow Fidel Castro); his work was used later to try and rationalise the Watergate scandal, the recent global banking crisis and many others. The Groupthink effect can cause the illusion of a heightened sense of morality; that the group is invulnerable and has 'right' on its side.

---

31 Moreover, the Semmelweis Reflex may kick in; our tendency to reject new evidence if it goes against our existing position.

32 Watch *Twelve Angry Men* starring Henry Fonda for an excellent examination of this.

33 When such groups are full of friendships, any disagreement may be seen as a slur on relationships and are therefore avoided.

Anyone not in that inner circle is stereotyped as weak or evil, or just plain wrong. The effect is similar to the cognitive bias known as the bandwagon effect – the tendency to do or think what everyone else does.

The results of Groupthink can be catastrophic, as the above examples demonstrate. Ideas and decisions are not fully thought through; counter-arguments are quickly closed down and evidence contrary to the group position is ignored; ergo, bad decision.

So how do we mitigate the effects of Groupthink? Janis later argued that it would help to create a culture where disagreement (especially disagreeing with the leader[34]) is not only possible but actually built in to the process, having subject-experts in attendance, and having follow-on meetings to check decisions after a cooling-down period. Following group facilitation methodologies (such as De Bono's *Six Thinking Hats*) may help create the norm that looking systematically at several angles of the issue in turn, and not just agreeing with the boss, is expected[35].

Not all researchers agree with Janis, and Groupthink certainly doesn't happen in every group with a directive leader. Simply being aware that it can happen if a certain set of conditions are there may be enough to prevent it having an adverse impact on group decisions.

Focusing on process (*how* the group works) as much as content (*what* it's there to do) appears to be the key. This rarely seems to happen, despite research showing that when it does – i.e. when groups decide on a problem solving strategy before leaping into solving it – they tend to make better decisions[36]. It's hard not to come to the conclusion that when it comes to decision making in groups, less is more.

34 Furthermore, it helps if the leader withholds stating their opinion until later in the process (as with coaching).

35 Janis also specifically states that just getting the boss to come up with the answer is not the, erm, answer.

36 Hackman (1990). I often use the analogy on teambuilding sessions of writing an essay under exam conditions – spending a bit of time up-front to decide *how* you are going to answer the question before you put pen to paper usually results in a better answer.

chapter 17

high performing teams

So far we've looked at definitions of teams, how they form, and what psychology tells us about how teams (and the individuals within them) tend to behave. This leads neatly into the question that most managers are concerned with: what makes a team high performing?

what makes a team high performing?

The literature on high performing teams (HPTs) is vast. It defines such a team as one that has a common aspirational purpose, one where its members use their knowledge of each other and their complimentary skills to exceed expectations.

Arguably the seminal work on HPTs is Katzenbach and Smith's *The Wisdom of Teams*[1], in which the authors define what makes a team high performing after analysing the common factors across a variety of organisations and sectors – and discovered some basic disciplines that united them all.

---

1 Summarised by the same authors in *The Discipline of Teams* (2008).

common purpose

Firstly, HPTs identify with a common purpose. This is an overarching idea or vision of what the team is there to achieve. This is not a mission statement imposed from on high, but one that has been shaped (and therefore owned) by the team itself. Without it, individuals act as individuals – they may well meet their individual targets, but the synergy, collaboration and collegiality is lost.

Perhaps the overarching purpose of the group has been set by senior management, but to get true ownership the Psychological Manager needs to help the team translate it into a more local one that makes sense 'on the ground'. This may take time and effort, but the resulting commitment to the cause is ultimately worth it.

This common purpose is more than just a goal or set of goals that can't be performed by individuals alone. It is focused on the future and what you and your team want it to look like. It should give a team and the individuals within it a sense of team identity and spirit (therefore fulfilling one of Adair's fundamental needs – see Chapter 15). It is the glue that binds the team together and keeps team members focused on the bigger picture when the day job threatens to swamp them[2].

At its best, it also provides a deeper sense of meaning; to badly misquote Nietzsche, 'he who has a *why* can put up with almost any *how*'. Of course this was explored in some depth in Chapter 10 on motivation theory – it's the deeper, more intrinsic elements of a job that tend to provide sustainable job satisfaction and therefore higher performance.

goals and objectives

HPTs also have their own set of goals and objectives – not merely the collective goals and objectives of their constituents. As we discussed earlier, these need to be SMART, with tangible deliverables that achieve what the team as a whole was created to achieve, and to know that collectively they are on track.

While they should be different and separate from individual goals to create the sense of a separate team entity, these team goals must resonate as loudly to each individual as their own individual ones. Perhaps the best way of doing this is to ensure that most of the individual goals dovetail with the team ones.

---

2 You may have heard of the classic fable of someone meeting four bricklayers; when asked in turn what they were doing, the first says 'Laying bricks', the second 'Building a wall', the third 'Creating a cathedral' and the fourth, who's obviously read Katzenbach and Smith, 'Serving God'. I'll leave you to guess which one is supposed to be more motivated.

Without this clear link from individual goals to team goals to team purpose that the individuals are committed to, the team members start behaving as independent units rather than a high performing team[3].

complimentary skills and knowledge

HPTs have a mix of different but complimentary skills and knowledge spread among their members. These may relate to technical skills and knowledge, interpersonal or behavioural styles and problem solving or decision making skills. They may be able to interchange their roles when needed and be comfortable trying different styles and ways of working that may go against preference. This area is covered in some depth in Chapter 19, using the frameworks of Belbin's Team Roles © and the Myers Briggs Type Indicator © as ways of understanding the particular behavioural styles and preferences of your team. In any event, particular skills and knowledge may not necessarily be there at the start; high performing teams take the opportunity to learn and develop as they go along.

identifying strengths

Related to this is the growing area of identifying and using strengths as a way of getting teams to perform at their best. Understanding how the individual strengths that people demonstrate can be harnessed collectively for the group is both motivational and helps create team identity, as they are channelled towards achieving the common purpose. Strengths-based questionnaires and activities are increasingly used in team settings as part of teambuilding sessions to provide focus, energy and an atmosphere of positivity.

content and process

Linking to the previous heading, HPTs demonstrate a commitment to understanding the difference between content and process, and treat them both with equal importance. As with team formation (see Chapter 15), this is the *what* and the *how*.

In such teams tasks become learning interventions with review systems in place to extrapolate learning, and constructive feedback is given and received. Conflict is dealt with, rather than ignored or denied and left to fester, and team

3 If you can help create some of the individual goals so they have an element of 'collaborating with other team members' about them, so much the better. Sometimes these may feel like an artificial creation, but building some degree of interdependency can really help the commitment to team ethos, as long as it is specifically defined. 'Work with John on this project' simply doesn't cut it.

members take the opportunity to practise their peer coaching skills. Mistakes are used as learning opportunities and managed risk is embraced rather than avoided. At its best, the team will agree the ground rules for team operation; who will do what tasks, deadlines and milestones, decision making procedures and review/feedback mechanisms.

mutual accountability

Finally, according to Katzenbach and Smith, HPTs hold themselves mutually accountable. If the first four points are addressed, then this will happen as a natural consequence – if we have a common purpose, specific, clear objectives, a complimentary range of knowledge and skills and a focus on *how* the work is done rather than merely *what* is done, then each team member tends to subscribe to the cause, with a resulting increase in trust and commitment. This means that each member is prepared to take the lead when necessary, not merely relying on the team leader or manager to automatically take the helm[4].

---

4 You may have heard of the 'flying geese' analogy in management literature or on courses. A skein of geese fly in a V shape because it is efficient; each goose rides the slipstream of the one in front and therefore gets more uplift and less wind resistance (a similar principle is used by Formula One racing drivers, tucking in close behind the car in front). Flying this way, a skein can fly up to 70% further. However, the goose at the front gets knackered very quickly, so the leader is rotated periodically.

chapter 18

managing the virtual team

Of course, managing your team is made much easier if the team are all together. Increasingly, however, this is not the case. New ways of working – flexitime agreements, remote working, multi-site (even multi-continent) teams – together with technological improvements in communications, mean that we don't always regularly see our team in the flesh. So what can the manager of geographically dispersed teams or those with a variety of flexible working arrangements do to manage their team effectively and ensure that it's still high performing?

In many respects, managing a virtual team is similar to managing one that's all in the same place. All of the theories, principles and practices we've already outlined still apply. It's just harder to spot them and potentially harder to deal with them.

the rise of flexible working

It's worth pointing out that there are many advantages to organisations in allowing flexibility of working practices, or indeed in having members of your team located elsewhere. Flexible working promotes goodwill with staff, and may be more productive for some people who don't need the structure of a nine to five office location[1]. This blended working style, or 'Martini working'[2], doesn't suit everyone, but for many it leads to higher output and greater job satisfaction.

In fact, increasing pressures on organisational space and environmental sustainability concerns have already led to increased hotdesking and flexible working as the norm, built into the strategic plans of estates departments countrywide. Add to this the advantages of having members of your team located near, say, a particular client base or embedded in various parts of the organisation, and the idea of having your team cosily located in one room sounds quite dated[3].

This has very real implications for the way in which you manage. The jobs where we assume someone isn't at work if they're not at their desk are getting fewer and fewer; they may turn up at 10am but have been working on their [*insert mobile device of choice*] in a coffee shop for the last two hours. Command-and-control 'presenteeism' surely now can't be the best way to manage in this permanently connected world – if indeed it ever was. Our mobile device is now our office, and it is about to become the primary way we access the internet. As such, for many jobs, *where* someone works is fast becoming irrelevant – all that matters is the output.

This raises important questions. What is now expected of the manager of a virtual or flexible team? How does this fit culturally with the rest of the organisation? What performance management methods make the most sense in this more fragmented workplace? And, of course, how do we maintain the sense of team when our co-workers work mainly from home or are located in Brazil[4]?

be flexible

While there should always be a clear theme and authenticity to your management style, it's no longer possible to treat all the members of your team the same in

---

1 Or spending two hours every day with their nose stuffed into another commuter's armpit.

2 Working 'Any place, anytime, anywhere' – not with a stiff drink.

3 There's a further pressure here in the rise of Generation C, the cohort now leaving school and university (also called Millennials). 'C' stands for connected, content-driven, communicating, computerised, and other words beginning with C. This way of flexible, permanently connected working is all they know and what they'll expect when they come and work for you.

4 Or even Basildon, or a few streets away. The actual distance seems to matter less than the fact that there *is* a distance.

terms of working styles and practices. To some extent this is one of the themes of this book – increasing your managerial toolkit so you can deal flexibly with varying degrees of skill and will in your teams – so maybe it's not such a huge leap. With mobile connections the norm, we now also have to consider the where and the when of working, not just the what and the how, and this may need to be tailored to each individual in your team.

Many organisations have introduced guidelines that place the onus on the manager to demonstrate why a member of their team can't work flexibly or remotely, as opposed to the team member having to make the business case for it. Indeed, at the time of writing it's a legal obligation to consider flexible working requests if it's at all possible. This calls for flexibility on behalf of the manager and acknowledgement of resulting protocol from the individual concerned to ensure the arrangement is satisfactory to both parties and the wider team. Work-life flexibility is the new work-life balance!

manage performance

Managing performance effectively becomes even more important. And not just performance – having clear rules of engagement and ground rules for behaviour are vital. Discussions and agreement should take place to clarify how the team will operate – both those who are mainly office based and those who work more remotely or virtually. Parameters include communication methods and frequency, 'checking-in' expectations, how to share progress and more personal updates, how decisions are made and any differences resolved. Review them regularly – what have you and the team learned about how to work in this way?

remote conversations

I've argued throughout this book that managing performance is primarily concerned with conversations. Work happens through relationships, and though technology can help with this it's all too easy to focus on the gadget and not the message. It's the *conversation* that's important, and with virtual teams you need to make a bigger effort to have those conversations to ensure shared clarity of purpose (individual and team) and targets/goals/objectives. This may include tangible deliverables and intangible outcomes or behaviours.

It's also important to remember that we miss out on many of the subtleties and nuances of language and non-verbal communication when we use email, tele-conferencing and, to a lesser extent, video-conferencing. As a result, misunderstandings are more likely to happen, and interpersonal differences and conflicts become harder to resolve and may drag on longer than is necessary or healthy[5].

Apart from these particular issues, the ways of managing the performance and development of an individual who works flexibly, or remotely, are the same as those already discussed in Section four. Goal setting, giving feedback, coaching and addressing an individual's motivational drivers are the key skills required; you just have to be more rigorous and structured in your approach as you don't always have the luxury of the spontaneous conversation. And remember that to some people, public recognition from their team members is an important motivator, so make the effort to celebrate individual success with the whole team.

build and maintain the sense of team

Perhaps the biggest challenge when managing a team, however, is to build and maintain the sense of team. I mentioned earlier that a large part of our learning comes from social interaction, and that such interaction fulfils a deep-rooted need in us. One of the dangers of flexible or remote working is that it can lead to team members feeling isolated and disconnected from the rest of the team and from its core purpose[6].

And this can be real, not merely imagined or perceived. One study found that distributed work groups led to fragmented communication, failure to return telephone calls or respond to enquiries from other team members, individuals being left off email distribution lists and, at worst, remote workers being viewed as part of the out-group[7] (see Tajfel's social identity theory in Chapter 16). The actual distance didn't seem to make any difference; it was the lack of the 'water cooler' type conversations and other spontaneous social exchanges that left people feeling out of the loop.

limitations of technology

The communication technology we use to enable this new way of working has its own limitations. Some researchers suggest that the lack of social and non-

5 Especially important when you're the boss. As I've said before, emotions are contagious and the strongest emotion is the one that gets noticed in a group. When the boss has the emotion, people pay extra attention to see what sort of a day they're going to have, because the ripple effect is heightened. We all prefer it when the boss is smiling, unless the boss is Jack Nicholson. When using technology to communicate, managers have to be even more careful to get the tone just right.

6 We don't get the hit of the 'You are my friend' chemical, oxytocin (Rock (2009)).

7 Armstrong & Cole (2002).

verbal cues in text-based communication methods increases the sense of anonymity and results in a state of 'deindividuation'. When this state happens, our characters and the characters of others are essentially depersonalised, and generally accepted norms of politeness and social etiquette fly out of the window[8].

Of course as such technology becomes the norm, we may well learn to adapt accordingly, but it's fair to say that such electronic relationships are more tenuous and fragile without our mirror neurons reinforcing the empathic understanding and flow of emotions of our fellow team members.

There may also be an additional effect. Walther (1996) in his 'hyperpersonal perspective' theory suggested that the limited cues that we do get when using new media are exaggerated as they're all we have to go on. Our impressions of others therefore become biased as we focus on the only things that are available to us.

So it's all too easy for remote workers to feel (and in many cases, be) misconstrued or even forgotten as part of the team. Of course, this effect is amplified if there are time, language and cultural differences between the team members. For more senior managers who may be trying to integrate several distributed teams into one coherent, strategic whole, the challenge can also be to mitigate the effects of each team having its own culture and norms, definitions of quality and acceptable behaviour and the like.

promoting the sense of team identity

All is not lost, however. While it's undoubtedly harder, there are many things that you as a manager can do to promote the sense of team identity when you have flexible or remote team members. Remember that in an organisation with a high degree of technical orientation (often the type of organisation that embraces distance working) people skills may be overlooked just when they are most needed[9].

spell it out

The first thing to do is to make everything explicit. Don't assume that everyone knows what's going on or is aware of how projects fit in with core purpose or the

---

8 Sproull & Kiesler (1986). Also compare this concept with Zimbardo's definition of deindividuation on page 146.

9 Kirkman et al (2002).

direction of travel. Spell it out and ensure that all your team members are aware of what each other is working on. As far as possible, create projects or working groups that mean individuals have to work together and find ways around the distance or different hours. Anything you can do to increase such connectivity will increase cohesion, team identity and increase the trust levels. It may help to explicitly reward collaborative efforts.

build trust

And talking of trust levels, this of course includes you as a Psychological Manager. In Chapter 10 we explored Douglas McGregor's theory X and theory Y. I'll assume by now it's pretty much understood that a manager who subscribes to theory X is going to have a hard time building trust in a multi-located team or one where individuals work at least partly remotely. Managing by trust, not control, brings the commitment of employees into sharp focus and allows them autonomy – often a key motivational driver.

Your role becomes one of helping to set goals and related deliverables – the role of your team members is to deliver those goals in their own way rather than by a set process[10]. Other researchers suggest that creating team interdependence on projects is especially vital in the first year of a team's existence; after that point enough of a team identity has been created through the sharing of ideas, communication and subsequent improvement in relationships (and therefore trust) for it to become a group norm[11].

regular events

It's also important to engineer regular formal and informal events. Schedule regular meetings, in person if possible, but via video-conferencing or tele-conferencing if not. Create social events to reinforce interpersonal relations and team bonding, and specifically help new team members become part of the in-group. Use social media where appropriate. And if you can, spend some of your budget on regular teambuilding sessions where everyone meets up face to face and spends quality time together, working on problem solving techniques, communication exercises or individual/team insight activities such as sessions built around team dynamics[12].

Finally, remember to take account of local sensitivities and styles, where necessary, and be culturally intelligent.

10 Bell & Kozlowski (2002).

11 Hertel et al (2004).

12 See Chapter 19.

chapter 19

teambuilding

understanding your team

Individuals within teams tend to have a mix of different and complimentary behavioural styles, preferences, knowledge and strengths – and this is particularly so in high performing teams. Understanding these differences and ensuring that they can be capitalised on are often the focus of teambuilding activities. Every team needs to take time out now and then to explore these differences. Teambuilding is an opportunity to develop self and team awareness and to use such awareness to channel efforts and commitment to the common purpose.

Stephen Covey calls this habit 7, 'Sharpen the saw'[1]. While his focus is on the individual, the same principle also works for the team; periodically taking time out to address needs and concerns, renewing energy, and understanding each other through activities and conversations helps provide a metaphorical caffeine hit.

1 In *The 7 Habits of Highly Effective People*. He uses the story of a woodcutter being so busy cutting down trees that he doesn't have time to make sure his saw is up to the job. According to Covey, it's the habit that allows the others to happen.

Teambuilding sessions are usually based around process, not content. There's obviously nothing wrong with getting the team together to discuss work-related issues, make decisions and monitor standards or discuss future direction and strategy – far from it. But the team that does only this content-related stuff and doesn't periodically review the 'how' – how the team operates – risks working with a blunt saw.

Such team events usually look at decision making processes by using activities and games, relationship building activities and 'getting to know you' sessions, and self/team insight using models of individual differences or strengths and how they impact on the work of the team.

Two of the most popular frameworks used in teambuilding sessions to help improve awareness of individual and team roles and styles are Belbin Team Roles © and the Myers Briggs Type Indicator (MBTI) ©, described below.

Belbin's Team Roles

If you can avoid the trap of assigning members of your team with labels (limiting at best, downright offensive at worst), then an understanding of the roles typically played within teams can be useful. Perhaps the best known – or at any rate most commonly used – is the framework developed by Meredith Belbin in the 1970s. Belbin found through making executives play team games[2] that these executives tended to take on particular roles within the team, with the balance of particular roles having a clear impact on the outcome. This seemed to have little to do with the individual abilities of the team members – it was the roles that they gravitated towards that had the biggest impact.

Belbin grouped the behaviours and contributions he saw into related clusters that he termed Team Roles. These have been developed through the intervening years into nine clearly defined roles; Belbin's premise is that successful teams have many of these roles covered by the team members.

It's true that people tend to gravitate towards playing particular roles in a team. You'll always have individuals who want to drive the proceedings and others who tend to be conscientious and focused on delivering a finished project on time, and as such it's all too easy to classify (and therefore limit) your team members with these labels. This is about preference, not necessarily ability.

Your job as a manager is to balance getting the best out of your team by helping and encouraging them to play to their strengths, while gently pushing them out of their comfort zones by encouraging and supporting them to try out

2 Probably not Twister.

new roles. It's not always an easy – or obvious – balance, and all too often the task delivery can take over, but it is worthwhile persevering. You'll end up with a far more flexible team in the long run – and one that is continually developing.

An added benefit of your awareness of the typical Team Roles the individuals in your team tend to play is that it may help you diffuse any tensions as they arise and before they become toxic. Understanding that the natural Resource Investigators may occasionally be annoyingly overoptimistic and therefore get on the nerves of the (typically) more anxious and worrying Completer Finishers is useful data!

There are many factors that go into determining our typical favourite roles. Elements of our personality such as whether our preference is for extraversion or introversion (see page 168) play a part, as well as anxiety tendencies. Our intellect will have an influence as will our values and motivations, our past experience and the requirements of our current job role or the task in hand. Most people therefore tend to have two or three 'default' Team Roles that they naturally slip into. Needless to say, you can identify your own typical roles through Belbin's questionnaire[3]. Many psychometric assessments of personality undertaken for selection or development purposes, such as 16PF © or the OPQ © include in their expert system (computer generated) report an approximation of Team Roles.

the nine Team Roles

These nine Team Roles are briefly described below:

- **Plants** tend to be creative problem solvers and are ideas-oriented. They can be adept at addressing complicated issues and may have a refreshing 'out from left-field' way of looking at the task in hand. However, they may tend to be less than practical, unlikely to be preoccupied with detail (equally cursed and blessed) and may not be the best at communicating or being collegiate, especially when they become wedded to their ideas. Plants like to have advocates, and work best with managers who appreciate and develop their talent.

  Most likely to say: 'There's no such thing as a problem without a gift for a genius such as I.'

  Least likely to say: 'Let's mull this one over for a few weeks while we sift painstakingly through all the details.'

- **Resource Investigators** are typically extravert communicators, who

3 www.belbin.com.

enthusiastically explore opportunities and develop useful networks. They are often good at keeping the energy of a group up, especially at the start of the project or meeting. Unfortunately this doesn't tend to last and they may lose interest. They are often better starters than finishers and may renege on arrangements. Resource Investigators like to be given a lot of leeway by their managers, and prefer ones with a focus on the bigger picture rather than the details.

Most likely to say: 'There's an opportunity here somewhere; I know a person who ...'

Least likely to say: 'Let's stick with this until it's finished.'

- **Co-ordinators**[4] help the group to clarify goals and expectations, and may help determine what particular decisions need to be made. They often appear confident, delegating tasks when needed (and sometimes at the expense of their own personal delivery). If the Co-ordinator role is performed clumsily, it may come across as manipulative or self-serving. Co-ordinators like to work for managers who accept their own drive towards management and view them as an equal.

  Most likely to say: 'Let's go back to the purpose of this meeting; is everyone in agreement?'

  Least likely to say: 'Would someone else like to take charge?'

- **Shapers** challenge, drive and provoke others in the team, pushing them to perform at their best. They often deal well (even thrive) under pressure and make brave decisions. This may sometimes be at the expense of others' feelings, becoming frustrated or annoyed if things don't go their way or if others don't seem to have the same drive as them. As a result, they may often need to apologise, which unfortunately they rarely do. Shapers work at their best with a manager who does not directly interfere but is there to give advice when asked.

  Most likely to say: 'What do you mean, it's not done yet?'

  Least likely to say: 'No need to apologise, I wasn't that bothered, really.'

- **Monitor Evaluators** take a strategic, overarching perspective on issues, tending to logically judge and weigh up the various options available. They may come across as being rather critical of others when detailing disadvantages of ideas or others' input. Not the most inspirational Team Role

4 Used to be called Chairman until the PC police took him outside and shot him.

if performed without careful attention to interpersonal skills, and may even gravitate towards negativity or cynicism. Monitor Evaluators work best for a manager who will consult with them and seek their advice.

Most likely to say: 'Let's sit back and take a long, hard, objective look at the options and their pros/cons.'

Least likely to say: 'Sod the logic, how do we really *feel* about this?'

- **Teamworkers** tend to be collegiate, co-operative, perceptive and diplomatic in groups. They focus more on the process than the content of the task at hand, using their listening and questioning skills to ensure all others are included, often reducing any group tensions along the way. This all may be at the expense of the task at hand, however, and they may come across as indecisive, easily manipulated or avoiding of conflict. Teamworkers like to work for decisive managers who know what they want from them and value the harmonious atmosphere they strive to facilitate.

  Most likely to say: 'Hey team, let's make sure everyone gets a chance to participate.'

  Least likely to say: 'I don't care what you think, we're in a hurry and this report won't write itself.'

- **Implementers** are usually disciplined, practical and pragmatic group members, taking the ideas of others and making them happen. They are often very action-orientated and can usually be relied on to deliver. Their pragmatism may sometimes come across as inflexible and they may appear closed to change. They prefer managers who know what they want and set out goals and expectations clearly.

  Most likely to say: 'With a bit of application and a lot of hard work, we'll get this working.'

  Least likely to say: 'Why don't we all have a lie down and look at this tomorrow?'

- **Completer Finishers** are at their best when they are looking for errors and omissions in documents or other outputs of the group. They tend to be conscientious and reliable, liking to close projects down and, erm, complete and finish them. They may worry or get tense when this doesn't seem to be happening and may take on the responsibility for delivery. They may tend towards perfectionism or even obsessional behaviour and may not always trust others. Completer Finishers work best for managers who value results and projects that are delivered on time and to budget.

Most likely to say: 'Let's go through this one more time – with luck we may be able to find and correct another error!'

Least likely to say: 'No need to check it, it's probably good enough as it is.'

- **Specialists**[5] are at their best when they are brought in as 'technical expert' on a specific part of a project. They often provide a narrow, skills based, clearly defined segment of knowledge. While their input is often useful, they tend to contribute on an often small part of the overall project and may not be interested in the bigger picture, ignoring anything that doesn't interest them. Specialists need managers who value the particular knowledge and skills they bring to the table, and who don't force them to do things outside their expertise.

  Most likely to say: 'It's funny you should say that. This just happens to be my bag ...'

  Least likely to say: 'I know it's nothing to do with me, but bring it on ...'

roles: the three categories

Belbin argues that these Team Roles are clusters of behaviour, rather than personality characteristics. He also groups them into three categories:

- **Action** Roles (Completer Finisher, Implementer, Shaper)
- **Social** Roles (Co-ordinator, Resource Investigator, Teamworker)
- **Thinking** Roles (Monitor Evaluator, Plant, Specialist).

using the Team Roles

So how can knowledge of these Team Roles help you?

It's certainly not advisable to use them as a key part of your selection criteria when building a team (there are too many other factors relating to personality, intellect, motivation and knowledge/experience to consider).

However, an awareness of the theory and the typical roles people prefer to play may help you put together working parties, facilitate meetings and projects better and simply recognise the value of individual differences and diversity in existing employees. It will help you ensure that any obvious gaps in your team are covered elsewhere or at least acknowledged and mitigated against.

In smaller teams, having an awareness of just what constitutes the three categories mentioned above may help to identify the glaring omissions. An

5 Joined once the others had got famous.

explanation of and exercises based around the theory can form a useful part of a teambuilding or strategy setting session; it will help you to clarify strengths and potential weaknesses within your team's dynamics and forewarn you of potential clashes of style.

Finally, of course, it may well help with your team's development planning. As in all personality models, knowing preferences should not be used as an excuse for poor performance or behavioural gaps[6] – rather it should be the starting point and springboard for further development.

Myers Briggs Type Indicator (MBTI)

The MBTI © is another useful framework to help you understand your team's dynamics and typical ways of communicating with each other and the outside world. It is one of the more useful models of personality in that it's both relatively easy to understand, and has practical implications for the way you manage the team and the individuals within it.

A brief overview of the theory and model follows; if you wish to explore this model with your team (and completing/getting feedback on the Indicator itself often forms part of a teambuilding session), then you'll need the services of a qualified practitioner.

Like all theories of personality, the MBTI (based primarily on Jungian theory) assumes that the important aspects of our personality are stable (as opposed to fixed) and tend towards consistency over time and situations. Jung discovered through his clinical work that in certain key areas of psychological functioning people tended to behave in predictable, consistent ways.

preferences: styles and patterns of behaviour

The central concept is one of *preference*; we have a preference for behaving in ways that we are most comfortable with, or in doing what comes naturally. This is not the only way we'll behave in any situation, but is the most common one and one which is (usually) when we are (re)acting at our best because we're most used to it.

These preferences are not abilities, being more concerned with style or patterns of behaviour rather than the quality of the end result. All preferences have equal value, and all have their strengths and weaknesses; an analogy with your preference for being left or right-handed is often used, which can lead to all sorts of interesting discussions about the genetic propensities of Jungian types[7].

6 So it's no use saying 'I know I didn't meet the deadline, but hey, I'm a Resource Investigator ...'

7 For any given definition of 'interesting'.

preferences: the four pairs

There are four bipolar pairs of preferences, and an individual is assumed to prefer behaving according to one of each pair of opposites over the other. This inevitably leads to the 'it depends on the situation' argument, but again we use our left hand for activities occasionally even if we have a preference for using our right.

This is primarily how a *type* approach to personality differs from a *trait* one; with a trait, it's assumed that we all have a bit of it to a greater or lesser extent (such as dominance); with type, it's an 'either-or' preference which can result in feeling labelled if used clumsily.

It's important to remember that we'll use all eight options at various times, but we tend to have our defaults when we're operating at our best. These four dichotomies are:

- Extraversion or Introversion (where we prefer to get and focus our energy)
- Sensing or INtuition (the type of information we focus on and trust)
- Thinking or Feeling (how we process information and make decisions)
- Judging or Perceiving (how we deal with the world around us)

The **Extraversion/Introversion** dichotomy is concerned with our orientation to the outside world and the energy exchange with it. Later definitions in the dictionary seem to have moved beyond the original Jungian definitions.

- **Extraverts** get their energy from the outside world of other people, activities and experiences, as a result being more action oriented, talkative and expressive, often appearing as if they are making it up as they go along. **Introverts** prefer to focus their energy more on their internal thoughts and reflections, tending to process information internally before offering any insights to the outside world. As such, they appear more reserved and self-contained.

The **Sensing/Intuition** dichotomy is concerned with how we perceive the world.

- Individuals with a **Sensing** preference rely mainly on facts or data coming in through the five senses, and as such tend to focus on what is real and tangible, often noticing details about events or data that those with a preference for Intuition have missed. Those with a preference for **Intuition** place more emphasis on the bigger picture; meanings, interpretations and possibilities.

They therefore may come across as abstract or theoretical. They often focus more on the future (and patterns from the past) than on the here and now.

The **Thinking/Feeling** dichotomy is concerned with how we prefer to process information and make judgements.

- Those with a **Thinking** preference base their decisions and thinking processes primarily on objective logic and 'if this, then that' cause and effect type reasoning. They work best when allowed to step outside a situation and dispassionately observe it from an objective, impersonal viewpoint. Those with a **Feeling** preference prefer to step inside the situation to experience any underlying motives and values and are often quick to find harmony and common understanding. Their own personal convictions are weighted heavily in any decisions they have to make.

The **Judging/Perceiving** dichotomy is concerned with how we deal with the extraverted part of life – the outside world.

- An individual with a **Judging** preference uses their Thinking/Feeling preference when dealing with the outside world, being likely to come to conclusions and achieving closure quickly. They often like to plan and organise activities. Those with a **Perceiving** preference use their Sensing/Intuition preference when dealing with the outside world, being open, curious and appearing more spontaneous, adaptable and open to change. They often prefer to keep options open, rather than being driven by a desire for closure.

According to the theory, therefore, an individual's MBTI Type comprises four letters; one from E/I, S/N, T/F and J/P respectively. The sum, however, is truly greater than the sum of the parts; as well as there being a description for each side of each pairing, there's an overall description for each one of the 16 possible combinations of these four preferences, which goes beyond the individual descriptions.

For example, an individual with an **ENTJ** preference[8] (Extraverted, Intuition, Thinking and Judging) will tend towards leadership positions, conceptualising and theorising what is possible and logically seeing tasks through to conclusion to achieve short and longer term objectives. Their extraverted nature means they are stimulated by interacting with others and will therefore be more likely to try to motivate and persuade those around them with their plans. However,

8 Guess which one I am ...

they may tend to make decisions too quickly (liking early closure) and may tend towards being rather directive or even critical.

using the MBTI

At an individual level, the MBTI is at its best when used as part of a self awareness exercise (for example as an element in a management development programme), with development planning or as part of a coaching intervention. It's also most commonly used as a teambuilding exercise, and it has many uses in such a setting:

- The individuals going through the teambuilding will get individual insight about themselves in a structured, often practical and engaging way.
- They'll learn about each other's preferences and understand (and hopefully value) the importance of individual differences. When done well, it can become a shared language that can live on and be built on long after the teambuilding intervention itself. For example, it can be used to explain why some people prefer information in advance of a meeting to make them more likely to speak up during it (Introverts) and why some people get frustrated at too much (to them, unnecessary) detail in documents or presentations (Intuitives).
- By adding up the number of **E** preferences, **I** preferences and so on in the team, you can determine an approximation of the overall team Type. While this is only a guide, it can help a team to understand why they come across to others in certain ways. You can then use the overall characteristics of that combined type to look at strengths and weaknesses of the team itself in terms of how it relates to the outside world.

An example may help here. I once did a team MBTI event with a group of IT workers; nine of the eleven members of the team reported themselves during feedback as ISTJs (Introvert, Sensing, Thinking and Judging).

ISTJs are practical, pragmatic, serious individuals, who prefer to work in a structured, logical way on structured, logical projects regardless of distractions or even of changing circumstances. This group certainly came across to others in this way, being perceived as reliable, conscientious and hardworking by their internal clients.

However, they tended to concentrate so much on logic and the details of the products that they were working on that they often failed to consider the impact their products and working styles had on the people they were working for –

and whether those products were still fit for purpose for the end user. In other words, there was a kind of Groupthink going on where no-one questioned the usefulness of what they were immersed in, or even checked with the clients to ensure they were doing what was actually wanted.

So the teambuilding exercise came up with three important insights:

- Recognition that this was the default tendency of the group – to get their heads down and work hard on projects they had never adequately questioned or checked with the organisation to see if these projects and products were useful. This helped the new manager of the department understand his main source of frustration; being an ENTJ he preferred to put his department's efforts into the context of more strategic goals and to get feedback from the end users as to the validity of their outputs. This outside awareness had hitherto been missing.
- It also helped the new manager understand why his team members communicated to him in the way that they did (full of detail and usually only in writing) and why the group tendency was to appear, at least, somewhat averse to change.
- The individuals within the team also developed more of an insight into their default patterns of working and prompted further development interventions (primarily facilitation and influencing/persuading skills development). It also helped them understand how to communicate more effectively with their boss.

In many ways, the MBTI keeps on giving. You can go (with expert help, of course) as deep as you want to. I've described above what may be achieved with a group in a one-day session, for example, but the theory itself goes into a lot more depth through analysis of type dynamics such as exploring our dominant, auxiliary, tertiary and inferior functions. This is probably more use in a coaching and individual development context – or at least in subsequent follow-on teambuilding exercises after a period of time getting to grips with the more basic elements of the theory.

On a final note, as with Belbin's Team Roles and like all theories, knowing your preferences should not be used as an excuse for justifying behaviour[9]. The real value of using the MBTI with your team is that it generates awareness of the world of individual differences and that alternative ways of behaving exist and could/should be explored – both at an individual and at a team level.

---

9 i.e. 'I don't do detail, I'm an N ...'

chapter 20

facilitating your team

facilitation skills

Good facilitation skills separate the theory Y manager from the autocratic, controlling theory X (see Chapter 10), and the Psychological Manager has a range of facilitation tools and techniques at their disposal.

When you act as an empowering coach, you're using facilitation skills; here we can build on coaching skills and take the same fundamental approach to problem solving or decision making with the team. Indeed, the GROW model of coaching applies just as well in the group setting and is often used as the basis for action learning sets or peer coaching circles, for example[1]. I said in Chapter 13 that 'coaching is an exercise in facilitation, not teaching or directing'. They are pretty much the same thing.

In many organisations there's an increasing trend to facilitate rather than chair meetings in the traditional sense, and this has led to more creative output from

1 I often use the GROW model as a framework for the whole facilitation session, and use the tools and techniques about to be described as ways of understanding Reality and generating Options.

those meetings. Some of the most successful high performing teams skill all their members with facilitation techniques in order to share and rotate the facilitation of their meetings, resulting in improved co-operation, commitment and buy-in to the outcomes and personal development of the individuals concerned.

To *facilitate*, then, simply means to make something easier, using a range of skills and methods to bring out the best in an individual or groups or a situation. It's different from training or presenting, as in those interventions the aim is to pass on knowledge, and the trainer or presenter is typically responsible for both the content and the process of the intervention. In facilitation, much like in coaching, the facilitator is responsible for the process, while the group collectively (which may or may not include the facilitator) remains responsible for the content or output. Such facilitators have to be credible, calm, empathic, challenging and structured while being able to cope with ambiguity. And, above all, they have to learn to trust the process.

attitude

In Chapter 13 I said that so much of coaching is about your attitude rather than skills per se. Yes, using a coaching framework and having great rapport building, questioning and summarising/reflecting skills are important, but if you really don't subscribe to the philosophy that people have all the resources they need internally to solve their own problems, then you'll limit the effectiveness and impact of your coaching conversations.

This philosophy or attitude is just as important when acting as a true facilitator. Rather than teaching the group (often about demonstrating how very clever we are) the skilled facilitator trusts that the group, if properly channelled, can come up with (often better) solutions together. A 'pure' facilitator, just like the 'pure' coach, doesn't give any advice or solutions whatsoever, but uses Socratic questioning or other techniques to enable the group to come up with the answers themselves. In practice, of course, this depends on the situation, and if you are the manager of the group then giving your opinions at finely tuned moments may be helpful[2].

levels of activity

When you're facilitating a discussion with your team it's helpful to remind yourself that in any group discussion there are three distinct levels of activity.

2 Do remember that when you are the boss, your opinions carry more weight (no matter how you try to diffuse this) and giving your opinions too early will just close down the debate or result in Groupthink.

Often the group is concerned only with one – and bad facilitators focus only on one – the *content*. The *process* is the responsibility of the facilitator. There's also one more level of activity to consider – and again this is the responsibility of the facilitator – the *climate*.

The climate concerns the feelings, energy levels, relationships and past history of the group members. It's important because the climate has a large impact on the group's behaviour, and as a consequence on whether the content (what the group is there to achieve) is actually achieved.

Good facilitators concern themselves with all three levels of activity, but they are likely to add most value by concentrating on process and climate. To do so they have to act like a lighthouse – constantly sweeping the room picking up on energy levels, relationships and non-verbal clues. Their role is to clarify, summarise, question, draw out quieter members, steer, challenge and feed back – and perhaps only then, as in coaching, offer their own ideas[3].

advance planning

As facilitator, a bit of advance planning is vital. We'll assume that, as manager, you know what the meeting is for, but clarifying in advance what you want as an outcome (and if necessary in the meeting steering the group towards this insight when setting objectives) will ensure you're more likely to get there. You may want to think about:

- what you want out of the discussion
- what ground rules are needed[4]
- the room/equipment logistics
- the history of the group and any previous experience of meetings
- any pre-existing vested interests or 'fixed' positions from group members.

Again the GROW model (see Chapter 13) is a useful framework for structuring a session, since the Goal element requires you to determine what success looks like by the end of the session. There are a few tools and techniques that are useful for helping determine current Reality and generating Options. Even if you're not structuring your session around GROW, they can still be used to pull out the parameters of a problem or to look at an issue from a variety of perspectives.

---

3 You can't push the river, but you can help to steer it towards the sea ...

4 Ground rules I tend to insist on are: challenge is welcome if constructive; build on ideas rather than mere blind disagreement; equal participation; and the challenging of the breaking of these ground rules.

overcoming cognitive biases

First, though, it's worth mentioning why a focus on the process of facilitation is important – without a few tools and techniques up our sleeve we (and our teams) tend to fall into one or several of the cognitive biases that blight our decision making. A few of these have already been mentioned – fundamental attribution error, group polarisation and Groupthink to name just three. There are many others: confirmation bias means people ignore evidence that contradicts their existing beliefs; while loss aversion makes us way too cautious and anti-risk.

Kahneman (2011) suggests that decision makers ask 12 key questions to mitigate the effects of the more common biases:

- Is the team motivated by self interest? (self interested bias)
- Are we in love with our proposal? (affect heuristic bias)
- Did we have adequate dissent? (Groupthink)
- Have we been overly influenced by past successes? (saliency bias)
- Have we included credible alternatives? (confirmation bias)
- Do we have the right data? (availability bias)
- Where did the data come from? (anchoring bias)
- Are we assuming success in one area means success in all? (halo effect)
- Are we too bound by history? (sunk-cost fallacy)
- Are we overly optimistic? (optimist bias)
- Is the worst case bad enough? (disaster neglect)
- Are we being too cautious? (loss aversion bias)

The problem with cognitive biases is that when they're happening we are unaware of them, and the fact that we are aware they might happen isn't enough. What can help is a systematic process for problem solving and decision making, and we'll now look at some of the more widely used ones.

gaining fresh perspectives: six facilitation techniques

By using these six facilitation techniques you as a manager will be able to make the most out of your meetings and teambuilding sessions by focusing on process instead of merely content. With these tools in your managerial toolkit you're not only showing leadership (good facilitation skills are at the heart of leadership) but will also be bonding your team together in effective decision making and problem solving processes.

brainstorming

Brainstorming – a useful process for 'freewheeling' ideas without the fear of being judged[5] – is in common use and no doubt you've used it at some stage. It's worthwhile, however, to briefly review the rules.

Brainstorming originated in the 1930s as a creative problem solving method in the advertising world. After a five-minute warm up using the brainstorming process on something totally unrelated, the facilitator poses a specific question or problem, and the group throw out ideas. The focus is on quantity, not quality; the idea is to generate as many ideas as possible in a fixed period of time. All ideas are welcome and captured in some way (usually on a flipchart).

No evaluation or critique of the ideas is allowed at this stage – the more people feel free to just give the first idea that comes to them without judgement, the more ideas tend to be generated and the more creative or unusual those ideas tend to be. As ideas get increasingly radical, there's a greater chance of something truly original emerging.

The facilitator should keep the atmosphere light, high energy, non-judgemental and fun, with the speed of responses being critical to prevent internal 'vetting' of ideas. Once a long list of ideas has been generated, the group then agrees a process for evaluating or voting on the ideas. The facilitator could encourage group members to combine ideas to see what emerges.

nominal group technique

The nominal group technique is a version of brainstorming where the group writes anonymous ideas on slips of paper that all go into a hat. The facilitator then reads out each idea to the group which is then voted on. The top ranked ideas are then discussed in further detail and final options ultimately agreed.

clustering

Another 'simple but good' technique is clustering. Have a clear discussion topic in mind (say, 'what does the topic of performance management cover?') and distribute a load of post-it notes. The team then write each idea or answer

5 If there's one thing that gets in the way of creativity, it's the fear of being made to feel silly.

they have on a separate post-it and stick them to a wall when all have finished. After that get the group to start clustering them together into meaningful 'lumps' or categories, and then invite the group to give each category a label.

force-field analysis

Force-field analysis is a technique most often used to help a group decide between options or decide on a particular course of action. It's a way of visualising the forces that influence a particular situation – either helping it (drivers) or not (restraining factors).

This technique was originally developed by Kurt Lewin, whom we met before when looking at group definitions. Lewin was coming at this from a social psychological perspective in that he defined the 'field' as a dynamic personal construct in the mind. This way of looking at an issue has been generalised to any situation that has factors for and against it.

As an example, take an individual's performance on a task. If you visualise an iron bar floating in space and label it, say, 'Team performance on [*a specific task*]'[6], there will be factors or 'forces' holding it up that are driving that individual's performance on the task (motivation, enthusiasm, some prior experience) and forces that are restraining the bar or stopping it from colliding with the European Space Station (lack of specific training, lack of goal clarity).

Using this technique with your group you can get them to identify drivers and restrainers on a particular issue, and once identified use brainstorming techniques to generate ideas for capitalising on existing drivers or deciding on new ones – and mitigating the effects of the restrainers.

PEST analysis

Originally designed as a methodology for conducting market research, a pest analysis (also called pestle or steeple) can be used to assess a range of factors that may have a bearing on a particular situation. PEST stands for:

- Political: legislation (current and anticipated), regulatory bodies and processes, consumer law, tax policies, health and safety and employment law, trading standards and political stability at home or abroad, environmental concerns.
- Economic: local and worldwide economic situation, trade cycles, interest, inflation and tax rates, international targets and quotas.

6 This is just the way I do it – bear with me ...

- Social: trends and demographics, media, fashion, ethnic trends, ethical issues, attitudes and public opinion.
- Technological: research and development activity, communications and computing innovations, general technological changes, manufacturing techniques and capacities, intellectual property and patents.

This technique is most often used as a template for ensuring that an adequate range of factors have been considered when writing strategy.

De Bono's Six Thinking Hats technique

A useful way of focusing thinking and exploring a variety of perspectives on a complex issue is Edward de Bono's *Six Thinking Hats* ® technique. This is a method of parallel thinking.

In his book[7] De Bono uses the analogy of four people looking at the outside of a house, with each looking at a different side. All have a different view, and all are correct when they describe what they see. Parallel thinking posits that all four should look at the front of the house to describe it, and then all go to the side, then the back, etc. In this way all four people have the same experience and see the house in the same four ways. All ways are therefore considered by everybody, reducing any disagreement about what's in front of them and taking away the need to display egos by deconstructing other people's viewpoints.

The 'hats' analogy is a way of ensuring there is a structured way of going round the house(s), so to speak. Each of the six hats represents a way of thinking about or looking at an issue. When a group metaphorically 'wears' one of the hats, they are all thinking about the same aspect of the problem together, and the idea is that the group thinks about that problem in a sequence, defined and determined by the colour of the hat. As such, it is a convenient mechanism for the group to quickly 'switch gears' and not get entrenched in a particular way of thinking.

These hats are described as follows:

- The **Blue hat** is the one the facilitator wears, and is the only one that an individual 'owns'. It is the one that looks at the process of the group, directing the flow of the conversation and the sequence of the hats, effectively 'managing' the thinking process.
- The **White hat** focuses on facts, data and trends. It considers any gaps in the data, and is essentially neutral and objective, with no interpretation.

7 De Bono (1999) *Six Thinking Hats*. London: Penguin.

It is often used at the beginning of a process as a context-setting device.

- The **Yellow hat** is the optimistic, constructive viewpoint, concerned with looking at the benefits and positives of the situation. It covers both the logical and practical and the visionary and aspirational. From this position comes concrete proposals.
- The **Black hat** is the opposite, concerned with the pessimistic viewpoint; what could go wrong, why it might not work and highlighting weak points. It is cautious, deals in risk identification and is often the most used (and abused).
- The **Green hat** is the creative one, looking at all the possibilities without reason or judgement (similar to the brainstorming idea). It is about growth, options and alternatives and under this hat suggestions are made, often provocatively.
- The **Red hat** is the one that addresses emotions and gut reactions, again, without judgement. When wearing this hat the group tries to consider how others will react emotionally. It legitimises feelings and makes them visible.

It's important to recognise that these hat descriptions describe essential thinking positions[8], not individuals. No hat is better than the others and all are necessary when considering a particular problem. The idea is that the facilitator (wearing the Blue hat) determines the sequence and moves the discussion on to consider another aspect.

In other words, 'Let's all now consider what could go wrong with this idea' is the facilitator requesting everyone to don the Black hat at the same time, generating ideas from the pessimistic viewpoint until moved on by the facilitator. The facilitator may then move the group to wear the Green hat, generating ideas and alternatives. What's important to the process is that the whole group wears the same hat at the same time, as opposed to assigning different people different hats for the duration – which does not lead to full creative potential and can end up unfairly stereotyping individuals.

So the *Six Thinking Hats* technique provides a roadmap for a structured, fully participative meeting or decision making process. It frees people up to be creative in parallel, rather than getting stuck in rigid adversarial patterns of behaviour[9]. It's also fun to use!

---

8 This can be tricky as we have all met (or had to manage) the individual who habitually wears the Black hat.

This is one of those models that really benefits from either reading the book (his, not mine) or attending a training course.

appreciative enquiry

This last technique is rooted in the positive psychology movement (see Chapter 2). Appreciative enquiry is, in group facilitation terms, a practical way of drawing out what's already going well and how any related strengths can be further capitalised on by applying them to other areas of work.

An analogy often used is to take the example of getting 8 out of 10 on a test. Our natural reaction is to focus on the 2 we got wrong and work out ways of developing that area. The strengths and positive psychology movement turns this on its head, suggesting that it's more motivational and probably more value adding if you work out what you did well on the 8 you got right and do more of it. It's more likely to result in real change because we like working on what we're already good at.

In group facilitation, then, appreciative enquiry is about facilitating the group to draw out what's going well in a certain sphere of work (say customer service or interdepartment communication) and to:

- identify what that actually looks, sounds and feels like (*Discover*);
- imagine what and how more can be done of those strengths and how that can be translated into other areas in the future (*Dream*);
- work out what needs to happen to make it happen (*Design*);
- then implement that plan (*Deliver*).

This process is motivational and high energy because it fires up all those feelgood chemicals – and there's nothing like talking about success to make a group more cohesive and committed. It works because it plays on our need for status and relatedness.

section checklist

The essence of this section is that a 'team' is more than just the sum of its parts. It has an identity over and above the identities of its constituents and it needs as much attention as any of them. As well as our need for meaningful work we have a need to be part of something bigger than ourselves, to feel we belong and fulfil a large part of our social identity. Historically, to do so gave us evolutionary advantage and the vestiges of that advantage stays with us in our desire to be part of the in-crowd, helped along by chemical and hormonal 'caffeine' hits. Your job as team manager is to bring clarity, structure and – above all – purpose to it.

As a Psychological Manager you now have a rudimentary understanding of the psychology of individual differences, how to help your team achieve their goals and how to motivate them to higher performance.

We can now add to that the understanding of the processes groups go through when forming, the psychological processes that seem to occur with depressing regularity in groups and how you can facilitate high performance in the team as a whole. This understanding is even more necessary with the increasing fragmentation of work groups and the rise of the flexible worker; the virtual team is fast becoming the norm.

So this section gives you a rudimentary understanding of psychology to help to manage your team more effectively. Like the coaching and feedback models described in Section four, many of the tools and techniques described here are useful transferable skills beyond your own team setting. I hope you find them useful. Repeat once a day until symptoms subside.

the psychological manager:

- Is aware that their team has a separate identity over and above the individual identities and foibles of its members.
- Acknowledges that being part of a team taps into deep-rooted desires and drives, forming an integral part of an individual's identity.
- Balances the needs of the tasks at hand, the individuals in their team and the team as a separate entity.
- Understands the stages groups tend to go through when first forming or after going through radical change: forming, storming, norming and only then truly performing.

- Has a broad understanding of the psychology of groups and what can be done to mitigate some of the least desirable consequences.
- Is familiar with the concept and the five parameters of the high performing team.
- Is aware that there are additional considerations to be made and strategies to take when managing a virtual team or one where members work remotely or flexibly.
- Understands the importance of regularly taking time out to 'Sharpen the saw' and review group processes such as decision making, communication and problem solving as well as clarifying individual strengths and weaknesses.
- Values the individual differences within their team and commissions interventions to help all the team to understand them and their implications.
- Regularly practises and develops their facilitation skills, and encourages the same development in the whole team.

afterword

So there you have it. A (mostly) impartial take on what makes a manager a Psychological Manager – one who uses a knowledge of psychological theory and practice to have more effective, constructive and possibly challenging conversations with their staff.

I mentioned in the Introduction that this book was born out of my own sub-discipline of Occupational and Organisational Psychology, my own experience of managing people, and the training courses I deliver on management development related skills. What was initially going to be the course notes for some of the courses I was running grew, as the links and common themes between them made themselves clear.

As I've said elsewhere, it never ceases to amaze me how little training and development support the majority of managers get when they are suddenly faced with managing a team. Many simply try to manage people as if they are projects, with the actual management squeezed into the end of the day, if they have time or inclination to do it at all.

One of the aims of this book is to put the *people management* of, erm, management in its rightful place – as the most important thing a manager does. The attitude shift comes first, a pre-requisite for any skills development. The best people managers know how to have conversations and are not scared to give their staff a good listening to in order to get the best out of them. This book is designed to give its readers the tools, techniques and background knowledge to do just that.

I also mentioned that people learn in different ways. Some will be drawn to reading a book like this, and others would prefer to attend a training course. This book was written to be a supplement to those courses, but is also designed to be read and understood on its own. By understanding both the theory and practice of performance-based conversations – goal setting, feedback, coaching and motivation – and understanding what happens when the collection of individuals become a team, you will become a better manager of people. Reading this book is the first step – the rest is just practice.

If, on reading this book, you think that managers in your organisation could benefit from improving their people management skills (and maybe attitudes), then please get in touch. I run a variety of workshops relating to the sections in this book, in addition to facilitating team events and individual/group coaching. Typical workshops include:

- developing yourself as a manager
- managing performance and development
- coaching skills for managers
- managing change
- building and developing your team.

Finally, thank you for sticking with this book until the end: I'd like to believe it was worth it. Writing it was both enjoyable and not a little cathartic! I'd be delighted to hear from you if you'd like to talk about any of the workshops mentioned above, or if you just want to make a comment or suggestion – or merely say hello.

www.thepsychologicalmanager.com
thepsychologicalmanager@gmail.com

references and influences

Adair, J. (2009). *Effective Teambuilding* (revised edition). London: Pan Books.

Adams, S. (1996). *The Dilbert Principle*. New York: Harper Business.

Argyris, C. (2008). *Teaching Smart People How to Learn*. Boston: Harvard Business Press.

Armstrong, D.J. & Cole, P. (2002). 'Managing Distances and Differences in Geographically Distributed Work Groups', from an original chapter in *Diversity in Work Teams: Research Paradigms for a Changing Workplace*, edited by Jackson, S. & Ruderman, M. (1995). Washington DC: American Psychological Association.

Arnold, J. & Randall, R. et al (2010). *Work Psychology* (5th edition). London: Prentice Hall.

Arthur, M., Claman, P. and DeFillippi, R. (1995). 'Intelligent Enterprise, Intelligent Careers', *Academy of Management Executive*, 9 (4) 7–19.

Asch, S.E. (1955). 'Opinions and Social Pressure', *Scientific American*, 193, 31–5.

Bach, R. (1977). *Illusions; The Adventures of a Reluctant Messiah*. Arrow Books.

Bailey, C. & Fletcher, C. (2002). 'The impact of multiple-source feedback on management development: findings from a longitudinal study', *Journal of Organisational Behaviour*, 23, 853–67.

Bandura, A. (1986). *Social Foundations of Thought and Action: A Social Cognitive Theory*. Englewood Cliffs, NJ: Prentice Hall.

Bayne, R. (1995). *The Myers Briggs Type Indicator*. London: Chapman & Hall.

Belbin, R.M. (1993). *Team Roles at Work*. London: Butterworth-Heinemann.

Bell, B.S. & Kozlowski, S.W.J. (2002). 'A typology of virtual teams: Implications for effective leadership', *Group and Organisation Management*, 27, 14–49.

Birch, A. & Hayward, S. (1994). *Individual Differences*. London; Macmillan.

Blanchard, K., Zigarmi, P. & Zigarmi, D. (2004). *Leadership and the One Minute Manager*. London: HarperCollins.

Blue Edge Motivation Questionnaire Qualification Workshop Workbook (2006). Blue Edge Consulting Ltd.

Botvinick, M., Jha, A.P., Bylsma, L.M., Fabian, S.A., Solomon, P.E. & Prkachin, K.M. (2005). 'Viewing facial expressions of pain engages cortical areas involved in the direct experience of pain', *NeuroImage*, 25, 312–19.

Bouchard & McGue (2003). 'Genetic and environmental influences on human psychological differences', *Journal of Neurobiology*, 54, pp 4–45.

Boyatsis, R.E. (1982). *The Competent Manager*. Wiley.

Boyes, C. (2010). *NLP Secrets*. London: HarperColllins.

Bray, R.M. & Noble, A.M. (1978). 'Authoritarianism and decisions of mock juries: Evidence of jury bias and group polarization', *Journal of Personality and Social Psychology*, 36, 1424–30.

Brewerton, P. & Millward, L. (2001). *Organizational Research Methods*. London: Sage Publications.

Brown, R. (1988). *Group Processes: Dynamics Within and Between Groups*. Oxford: Blackwell.

Burnard, P. (1994). *Counselling Skills for Health Professionals*. London: Chapman & Hall.

Burns, D. (1980). 'The Perfectionist's script for self-defeat', *Psychology Today*, November 34–51.

Burton, K. and Ready, R. (2010). *Neuro-linguistic Programming for Dummies*. West Sussex: John Wiley & Sons Ltd.

Centre for Coaching (2010). *Primary Certificate in Performance Coaching Manual*. Course held by the Centre for Coaching, London, 8 and 9 June 2010.

Charan, R., Drotter, S. and Noel, J. (2001). *The Leadership Pipeline*. San Francisco: Jossey-Bass.

Cheung-Judge, M. and Holbeche, L. (2011). *Organisation Development*. London: Kogan Page.

Chidambaram, L. & Tung, L.L. (2005). 'Is out of sight out of mind? An empirical study of social loafing in technology-supported groups', *Information Systems Research*, 16:2, 149–68.

Conway, N. & Briner, R.B. (2005). *Understanding Psychological Contracts at Work*. Oxford: Oxford University Press.

Costa, P.T. & McCrae, R.R. (1985). *The NEO Personality Inventory Manual*. Odessa, FL: Psychological Assessment Resources.

Covey, S.R. (2004). *The 7 Habits of Highly Effective People*. FranklinCovey.

Csikszentmihalyi, M. (1990). *Flow: The Psychology of Optimal Experience*. London: HarperCollins.

Cwir, D., Carr, P., Walton, G. & Spencer, S. (2011). 'Your heart makes my heart move: Cues of social connectedness cause shared emotions and physiological states among strangers', *Journal of Experimental Social Psychology*, 47, Issue 3, 661–4.

Dapretto, M., Davies, M.S., Pfeifer, J.H., Scott, A.A., Sigman, M., Bookheimer, S.Y. & Lacoboni, M. (2006). 'Understanding emotions in others: mirror neuron dysfunction in children with autism spectrum disorders', *Nature Neuroscience*, 9 (1): 28–30.

Dawkins, R. (1989). *The Selfish Gene* (2nd edition). New York: Oxford University Press.

De Bono, E. (1999). *Six Thinking Hats ®*. London: Penguin.

Eysenck, H. (1967). *The Biological Basis of Personality*. Springfield, IL: Thomas.

Eysenck, H.J. & Eysenck, S.B.G. (1964). *Manual of the Eysenck Personality Inventory*. London: ULP.

Eysenck, H.J. & Eysenck, S.B.G. (1975). *Manual for the Eysenck Personality Questionnaire*. London: Hodder and Stoughton.

Farr, J.L., Hoffman, D.A. and Ringenbach, K.L. (1993). 'Goal orientation and action control theory: implications for industrial and organisational psychology.' In Robertson, I.T. and Cooper, C.L. (eds) *International Review of Industrial and Organisational Psychology*, Vol 8. Chichester: John Wiley.

Festinger, L. (1957). *A Theory of Cognitive Dissonance*. Stanford, CA: Stanford University Press.

Flett, G.L. & Hewitt, P.L. (2002). *Perfectionism: Theory, Research, and Treatment*. Washington, DC: American Psychological Association.

Gallwey, T. (1986). *The Inner Game of Tennis*. Pan.

Gallwey, T. (2000). *The Inner Game of Work*. Texere.

Gardner, H. (1983). *Frames of Mind*. New York: Basic Books.

Gladwell, M. (2000). *The Tipping Point*. Little, Brown.

Gladwell, M. (2009). *Outliers: The Story of Success*. Penguin.

Goffee, R. and Jones, G. (2006). *Why Should Anyone Be Led By You?* Boston: Harvard Business School Press.

Goleman, D. (1998). *Working with Emotional Intelligence*. London: Bloomsbury.

Goleman, D., Boyatzis, R. and McKee, A. (2002). *The New Leaders*. London: Sphere.

Goodge, P. and Coomber, J. (2008). '360 feedback – once again the research is useful!' *Selection and Development Review*, Vol 24, No 2.

Hackman, J.R. (1990). *Groups That Work (and Those That Don't): Creating Conditions for Effective Teamwork*. San Francisco, CA: Jossey-Bass.

Handy, C. (1994). *The Empty Raincoat*. London: Arrow.

Hertel, G., Konradt, U. & Orlikowski, B. (2004). 'Managing distance by interdependence: Goal setting, task interdependence and team-based rewards in virtual teams', *European Journal of Work and Organisational Psychology*, 13, 1–28.

Herzberg, F. (2008). *One More Time: How Do You Motivate Employees?* Boston: Harvard Business Review Classics.

Hewstone, M., Ruibin, M. & Willis, H. (2002). 'Intergroup Bias', *Annual Review of Psychology*, 53, 575–604.

Hjelle, L.A. & Ziegler, D.J. (1981). *Personality Theories; Basic Assumptions, Research, and Applications*. McGraw-Hill International.

Honey, P. and Mumford, A. (1982). *Manual of Learning Styles*. Maidenhead: Peter Honey Publications.

Janis, I.L. (1972). *Victims of Groupthink*. Boston, MA: Houghton Mifflin.

Janis, I.L. (1982). 'Counteracting the adverse effects of concurrence–seeking in policy planning groups; Theory and research perspectives.' In Brandstatter, H., Davis, J.H. and Stocker-Kreichgauer (eds). *Group Decision Making*. London: Academic Press.

Jones, E.E. & Harris, V.A. (1967). 'The Attribution of Attitudes', *Journal of Experimental Social Psychology*, 3, pp 1–24.

Kahneman, D. (2011). 'Before You Make That Big Decision ...', *Harvard Business Review*, June 2011, pp 51–60.

Katzenbach, J.R. & Smith, D.K. (1993). *The Wisdom of Teams*. HarperBusiness.

Katzenbach, J.R. & Smith, D.K. (2008). *The Discipline of Teams*. Boston: Harvard Business Press.

Keyes & Haidt (eds) *Flourishing: Positive Psychology and the Life Well-lived*. Washington DC: American Psychological Association (pp 275–89).

Kolb, D. (1984). *Experiential Learning: Experience as the Source of Learning and Development*. Englewood Cliffs, NJ: Prentice-Hall.

Kirkman, B.L., Rosen, B., Gibson, C.B., Tesluk, P.E. & McPherson, S.O. (2002). 'Five challenges to virtual team performance: Lessons from Sabre Inc.', *Academy of Management Executive*, 16, 67–79.

Landsberg, M. (1999). *The Tao of Motivation*. London: Profile Books.

Landsberg, M. (2002). *The Tao of Coaching*. London: Profile Books.

Latane, B., Williams, K. & Harkins, S. (1979). 'Many hands make light the work: the causes and consequences of social loafing', *Journal of Personality and Social Psychology*, 37, 822–32.

Leclerc, G., Lefrancois, R., Dube, M., Hebert, R. & Gaulin, P. (1998). 'The Self-actualisation concept; A contest validation', *Journal of Social Behaviour and Personality*, 13, 69–84.

Leigh, A. & Maynard, M. (1995). *Leading your Team*. London: Nicholas Brealey Publishing.

Lewin, K. (1948). *Resolving Social Conflicts*. New York: Harper and Row.

Lewin, K. (1943). 'Defining the "Field at a Given Time"', *Psychological Review*, 50: 292–310. Republished in *Resolving Social Conflicts & Field Theory in Social Science*. Washington, DC: American Psychological Association, 1997.

Lord, W. (1997). *16PF5: Personality in Practice*. ASE, A Division of NFER-Nelson.

Luhan, W.J., Kocher, M.G. and Sutter, M. (2009). 'Group Polarization in the Team Dictator Game Reconsidered', *Experimental Economics*, 26–41.

Lundin, S.C., Paul, H. & Christensen, J. (2000). *Fish!: A Remarkable Way to Boost Morale and Improve Results*. London: Hodder and Stoughton.

McCauley, C.D. and Moxley, R.S. (1996). 'Developmental 360: how feedback can make managers more effective', *Career Development International*, Vol 1, No 3. pp 15–19.

McCrae, R.R. & Costa, P.C. (1987). 'Validation of the five-factor model across instruments and observers', *Journal of Personality and Social Psychology*, 52, 81–90.

Marinelli, L. and Andreas Mayer, A. (2003). *Dreaming by the Book: Freud's 'The Interpretation of Dreams' and the History of the Psychoanalytic Movement*. New York: Other Press.

Meister, J.C. and Willyerd, K. (2010). *The 2020 Workplace*. Collins Business.

Milgram, S. (1974). *Obedience to Authority: An Experimental View*. HarperCollins.

Moscovici, S. & Zavalloni, M. (1969) 'The group as a polarizer of attitudes', *Journal of Personality and Social Psychology*, 12, 125–35.

Myers Briggs Type Indicator Qualification Workshop Workbook. (1999). Oxford: Oxford Psychologists Press Ltd.

Myers I., Briggs, K. et al (1998). *MBTI © Manual*. Palo Alto: Consulting Psychologists Press, Inc.

Northstone, K. et al (2011). 'Are dietary patterns in childhood associated with IQ at 8 years of age? A population-based cohort study', *Journal of Epidemiology and Community Health*. Published online.

Peter, L.J. and Hull, R. (1969). *The Peter Principle: Why Things Always Go Wrong*. New York: William Morrow and Company.

Pratkanis, A.R. & Turner, M.E. (1994). 'Of what value is a job attitude? A socio-cognitive analysis', *Human Relations*, 47, 1545–76.

Radcliffe. S. (2008). *Future, Engage, Deliver*. Leicester: Matador.

Rock, D. (2009). *Your Brain at Work*. New York: HarperCollins.

Rogers, C.R. (1951). *Client-Centered Therapy*. London: Constable.

Rothwell, J.D. (2004). *In the Company of Others*. McGraw-Hill.

Rotter, J.B. (1954). *Social Learning and Clinical Psychology*. NY: Prentice-Hall.

Rotter, J.B. (1966). 'Generalised expectancies of internal vs external control of reinforcements', *Psychological Monographs*, 80 (609).

Rynes, S.L., Gerhart, B. & Minette, K.A. (2004). 'The importance of pay in employee motivation; Discrepancies between what people say and what they do', *Human Resource Management*, 43, 381–94.

Schein, E.H. (1988). *Organizational Psychology*. Englewood Cliff, NJ: Prentice-Hall.

Seligman, M. (1990). *Learned Optimism: How to Change Your Mind and Your Life*. Free Press.

Sheridan, C.L. & King, K.G. (1972). 'Obedience to authority with an authentic victim', *Proceedings of the 80th Annual Convention of the American Psychological Association*, 7: 165–6.

Sherif, M. & Sherif, C.W. (1969). *Social Psychology*. New York: Harper and Row.

Shoda, Y., Mischel, W. and Peake, P.K. (1990). 'Predicting Adolescent Cognitive and Self-Regulatory Competencies from Preschool Delay of Gratification: Identifying Diagnostic Conditions', *Developmental Psychology*, 26 (6): 978–86.

Sia, C.L., Tan, B. & Wei, K.K. (2002). 'Group Polarisation and Computer-Mediated Communication: Effects of Communication Cues, Social Presence and Anonymity', *Information Systems Research*, 13, 70–90.

Slater, R. (2010). *Team Management Secrets*. London: HarperCollins.

Slessenger, N. (2003). *How to Write Objectives that Work*. Guildford: Vinehouse Essential Ltd.

Sproull, L. & Keisler, S. (1986). 'Reducing social-context cues: electronic mail in organisational communication', *Management Science*, 32, 1492–512.

Steers, R.M. & Porter, L.W. (1991). *Motivation and Work Behaviour*. McGraw-Hill, Inc.

Steiner, I.D. (1972). *Group Processes and Productivity*. New York: Academic Press.

Stoner, J.A.F. (1968). 'Risky and cautious shifts in group decisions; the influence of widely held values', *Journal of Experimental Psychology*, 4, 442–59.

Syed, M. (2010). *Bounce: The Myth of Talent and the Power of Practice*. London: 4th Estate.

Tajfel, H. & Turner, J.C. (1979). 'An integrative theory of social conflict', reprinted in Austin, W. & Worchel, S. (eds), *The Social Psychology of Intergroup Relations* (2nd edition), 1985. Chicago: Nelson Hall.

Tajfel, H., Flament, C., Billig, M.G. & Bundy, R.P. (1971). 'Social categorization and intergroup behaviour', *European Journal of Social Psychology*, 1, 149–78.

Thomson, L.L. (2003). *Making the Team: A Guide for Managers*. Saddle River, NJ: Pearson/ Prentice Hall.

Tuckman, B. (1965). 'Developmental sequence in small groups', *Psychological Bulletin*, 63 (6), pp 384–99.

Warr, P. (ed) (2002). *Psychology at Work*. London: Penguin.

Whitmore, J. (2009). *Coaching for Performance* (4th edition). London: Nicholas Brealey Publishing.

Zimbardo, P. (2007). *The Lucifer Effect; Understanding How Good People Turn Evil*. New York: Random House.

* D I D 1 4 4 6 9 2 2 *

#0138 - 090516 - C0 - 210/148/10 - PB - DID1446922